Decrypting the
ENCRYPTION DEBATE
A Framework for Decision Makers

Committee on Law Enforcement and Intelligence Access
to Plaintext Information

Computer Science and Telecommunications Board

Division on Engineering and Physical Sciences

A Consensus Study Report of

The National Academies of
SCIENCES · ENGINEERING · MEDICINE

THE NATIONAL ACADEMIES PRESS
Washington, DC
www.nap.edu

THE NATIONAL ACADEMIES PRESS 500 Fifth Street, NW Washington, DC 20001

This activity was supported by award number 2015-3078 from the William and Flora Hewlett Foundation, award number 15-109219-000-HRS from the John D. and Catherine T. MacArthur Foundation, and award number CNS-1555610 from the National Science Foundation. Any opinions, findings, conclusions, or recommendations expressed in this publication do not necessarily reflect the views of any organization or agency that provided support for the project.

International Standard Book Number-13: 978-0-309-47153-4
International Standard Book Number-10: 0-309-47153-2
Digital Object Identifier: https://doi.org/10.17226/25010

Additional copies of this publication are available for sale from the National Academies Press, 500 Fifth Street, NW, Keck 360, Washington, DC 20001; (800) 624-6242 or (202) 334-3313; http://www.nap.edu.

Copyright 2018 by the National Academy of Sciences. All rights reserved.

Printed in the United States of America

Suggested citation: National Academies of Sciences, Engineering, and Medicine. 2018. *Decrypting the Encryption Debate: A Framework for Decision Makers*. Washington, DC: The National Academies Press. doi: https://doi.org/10.17266/25010.

The National Academies of
SCIENCES · ENGINEERING · MEDICINE

The **National Academy of Sciences** was established in 1863 by an Act of Congress, signed by President Lincoln, as a private, nongovernmental institution to advise the nation on issues related to science and technology. Members are elected by their peers for outstanding contributions to research. Dr. Marcia McNutt is president.

The **National Academy of Engineering** was established in 1964 under the charter of the National Academy of Sciences to bring the practices of engineering to advising the nation. Members are elected by their peers for extraordinary contributions to engineering. Dr. C. D. Mote, Jr., is president.

The **National Academy of Medicine** (formerly the Institute of Medicine) was established in 1970 under the charter of the National Academy of Sciences to advise the nation on medical and health issues. Members are elected by their peers for distinguished contributions to medicine and health. Dr. Victor J. Dzau is president.

The three Academies work together as the **National Academies of Sciences, Engineering, and Medicine** to provide independent, objective analysis and advice to the nation and conduct other activities to solve complex problems and inform public policy decisions. The National Academies also encourage education and research, recognize outstanding contributions to knowledge, and increase public understanding in matters of science, engineering, and medicine.

Learn more about the National Academies of Sciences, Engineering, and Medicine at **www.nationalacademies.org**.

The National Academies of
SCIENCES · ENGINEERING · MEDICINE

Consensus Study Reports published by the National Academies of Sciences, Engineering, and Medicine document the evidence-based consensus on the study's statement of task by an authoring committee of experts. Reports typically include findings, conclusions, and recommendations based on information gathered by the committee and the committee's deliberations. Each report has been subjected to a rigorous and independent peer-review process and it represents the position of the National Academies on the statement of task.

Proceedings published by the National Academies of Sciences, Engineering, and Medicine chronicle the presentations and discussions at a workshop, symposium, or other event convened by the National Academies. The statements and opinions contained in proceedings are those of the participants and are not endorsed by other participants, the planning committee, or the National Academies.

For information about other products and activities of the National Academies, please visit www.nationalacademies.org/about/whatwedo.

COMMITTEE ON LAW ENFORCEMENT AND INTELLIGENCE ACCESS TO PLAINTEXT INFORMATION

FRED H. CATE, Indiana University, *Chair*
DAN BONEH, NAE,[1] Stanford University
FREDERICK R. CHANG, NAE, Southern Methodist University
SCOTT CHARNEY, Microsoft Corp.
SHAFRIRA GOLDWASSER, NAS[2]/NAE, Massachusetts Institute of Technology
DAVID A. HOFFMAN, Intel Corporation
SENY KAMARA, Brown University
DAVID KRIS, Culper Partners, LLC
SUSAN LANDAU, Tufts University
STEVEN B. LIPNER, NAE, SAFECode
RICHARD LITTLEHALE, Tennessee Bureau of Investigation
KATE MARTIN, Center for American Progress
HARVEY RISHIKOF, Cybersecurity Legal Task Force, American Bar Association
PETER J. WEINBERGER, Google, Inc.

Staff

JON EISENBERG, Study Director and Senior Director, Computer Science and Telecommunications Board
KATIRIA ORTIZ, Associate Program Officer
SHENAE BRADLEY, Administrative Assistant
JANKI PATEL, Senior Program Assistant

---

[1] Member, National Academy of Engineering.
[2] Member, National Academy of Sciences.

COMPUTER SCIENCE AND TELECOMMUNICATIONS BOARD

FARNAM JAHANIAN, Carnegie Mellon University, *Chair*
LUIZ ANDRE BARROSO, Google, Inc.
STEVEN BELLOVIN, Columbia University
ROBERT F. BRAMMER, Brammer Technology, LLC
EDWARD FRANK, Cloud Parity, Inc.
LAURA HAAS, University of Massachusetts, Amherst
MARK HOROWITZ, Stanford University
ERIC HORVITZ, Microsoft Research
VIJAY KUMAR, Univ. of Pennsylvania
BETH MYNATT, Georgia Institute of Technology
CRAIG PARTRIDGE, Raytheon BBN Technologies
DANIELA RUS, Massachusetts Institute of Technology
FRED SCHNEIDER, Cornell University
MARGO SELTZER, Harvard University
MOSCHE VARDI, Rice University
KATHERINE YELICK, University of California, Berkeley

Staff

JON EISENBERG, Senior Director
LYNETTE I. MILLETT, Associate Director
SHENAE BRADLEY, Administrative Assistant
EMILY GRUMBLING, Program Officer
RENEE HAWKINS, Financial and Administrative Manager
KATIRIA ORTIZ, Associate Program Officer
JANKI PATEL, Senior Program Assistant

For more information on CSTB, see its Web site at http://www.cstb.org, write to CSTB at National Academies of Sciences, Engineering and Medicine, 500 Fifth Street, NW, Washington, DC 20001, call (202) 334-2605, or email the CSTB at cstb@nas.edu.

Acknowledgment of Reviewers

This Consensus Study Report was reviewed in draft form by individuals chosen for their diverse perspectives and technical expertise. The purpose of this independent review is to provide candid and critical comments that will assist the National Academies of Sciences, Engineering, and Medicine in making each published report as sound as possible and to ensure that it meets the institutional standards for quality, objectivity, evidence, and responsiveness to the study charge. The review comments and draft manuscript remain confidential to protect the integrity of the deliberative process.

We wish to thank the following individuals for their review of this report:

Kevin Bankston, Open Technology Institute,
Alvaro Bedoya, Georgetown University Law School,
James Emerson, iThreat Cyber Group,
Edward W. Felten, NAE,[1] Princeton University,
Eric Grosse, EHG Flight, LLC,
Joseph Lorenzo Hall, Center for Democracy and Technology,
Susan Hennessey, Brookings Institution,
John C. ("Chris") Inglis, U.S. Naval Academy,
Kenn Kern, New York County District Attorney's Office,

---

[1] Member, National Academy of Engineering.

Butler W. Lampson, NAS[2]/NAE, Microsoft Corporation,
Josiah Landers, Rockland County, New York, District Attorney's Office,
Bruce W. McConnell, EastWest Institute,
Deirdre K. Mulligan, University of California, Berkeley,
Ronald L. Rivest, NAS/NAE, Massachusetts Institute of Technology,
Peter Swire, Georgia Institute of Technology, and
Marcus C. Thomas, Subsentio, LLC.

Although the reviewers listed above provided many constructive comments and suggestions, they were not asked to endorse the conclusions or recommendations of this report nor did they see the final draft before its release. The review of this report was overseen by Robert F. Sproull, NAE, University of Massachusetts, Amherst. He was responsible for making certain that an independent examination of this report was carried out in accordance with the standards of the National Academies and that all review comments were carefully considered. Responsibility for the final content rests entirely with the authoring committee and the National Academies.

---

[2] Member, National Academy of Sciences.

Preface

Government access to the plaintext of encrypted communications and stored data presents difficult, important, and controversial issues that reveal conflicting values within the government and society at large. The debate over efforts to ensure that access is very polarized. Critics of government access, even as they acknowledge the importance of effective law enforcement, cite legal and practical objections, including risks to security, privacy and civil liberties, and U.S. commercial interests. Government officials acknowledge the value of encryption to protect privacy and confidential information but also express the need to be able to access information relevant to investigations when properly authorized.

To address these issues (Box P.1), the National Academies of Sciences, Engineering, and Medicine appointed the Committee on Law Enforcement and Intelligence Access to Plaintext Information (biosketches in Appendix A). It met four times in person to receive briefings from government, industry, and academic experts (listed in Appendix B) and also used these meetings, supplemented by conference calls and email discussion, to deliberate and develop this report.

To better inform the policy debate and future decision making, this report reviews how encryption is used, including its applications to cybersecurity; its role in protecting privacy and civil liberties; the needs of law enforcement and the intelligence community for information; technical and policy options for accessing plaintext; and the international landscape.

Because the concerns expressed by law enforcement officials at the federal, state, and local levels have been more clearcut and less nuanced

> **BOX P.1**
> **Statement of Task**
>
> A National Academies of Sciences, Engineering, and Medicine study will examine the tradeoffs associated with mechanisms to provide authorized government agencies with access to the plaintext version of encrypted information. The study will describe the context in which decisions about such mechanisms would be made and identify and characterize possible mechanisms and alternative means of obtaining information sought by the government for law enforcement or intelligence investigations. It will seek to find ways to measure or otherwise characterize risks so that they could be weighed against the potential law enforcement or intelligence benefits. The study will not seek to answer the question of whether access mechanisms should be required but rather will provide an authoritative analysis of options and trade-offs.

than the views offered by U.S. intelligence officials, who in contrast to law enforcement representatives have not vigorously advocated in public for exceptional access, this report not only gives greater attention to law enforcement needs but also discusses national security needs. The last chapter of the report provides a framework for evaluating policy or technical approaches for government access to plaintext. The committee intends that developing and debating answers to these questions will help illuminate the underlying issues and trade-offs and help guide future decisions about government access to plaintext.

Moreover, while it suspects there will always be disagreements over how to address the challenges presented by encryption, it is the committee's hope that this report will facilitate a frank conversation, involving all parties, about those challenges and alternative approaches to addressing them. The process of creating this report at times was challenging and required members of the committee to develop a deeper understanding of perspectives with which they did not always agree. But the process was also illuminating, and the committee hopes that the common vocabulary and broad context provided by this report, as well as the analytical framework, will make future conversations easier, more productive, and more likely.

The committee would like to acknowledge the William and Flora Hewlett Foundation, the John D. and Catherine T. MacArthur Foundation, and the National Science Foundation for their generous support for this project and in particular Eli Sugarman (Hewlett Foundation), Eric Sears (MacArthur Foundation), and Jeremy Epstein (National Science

Foundation) for their encouragement and support. It also thanks the National Academies of Sciences, Engineering, and Medicine staff who supported this project: study director Jon Eisenberg, associate program officer Katiria Ortiz, and administrative assistant Shenae Bradley.

> Fred H. Cate, *Chair*
> Committee on Law Enforcement and
> Intelligence Access to Plaintext Information

Contents

SUMMARY 1

1 INTRODUCTION 5
   Government Options, 9
   Scope and Context for Access, 12
   Evaluation Framework, 12

2 ENCRYPTION AND ITS APPLICATIONS 14
   What Is Encryption?, 15
   Designing Encryption, 18
   Applications of Encryption, 20
      Protecting Stored Files, 20
      Full Disk Encryption, 21
      Device Locking, 22
      Virtual Private Networks, 22
      Secure Web Browsing, 23
      Secure Messaging, 24
      Protecting Confidentiality in Cloud or Third-Party Computing, 25
   Encryption and the Expanding Cyber Threat, 25
      Cyber Threats, 27
      The Role of Encryption and Other Forms of Cryptography in Cybersecurity, 29
      The Limits of Encryption for Cybersecurity, 31

3	THE ROLE OF ENCRYPTION IN PROTECTING PRIVACY AND CIVIL LIBERTIES	32
4	INFORMATION NEEDS OF LAW ENFORCEMENT AND THE INTELLIGENCE COMMUNITY	36

    Goals of Law Enforcement Officials and Intelligence Analysts, 36
    The Volume and Diversity of Information Relevant to Law Enforcement and the Intelligence Community, 37
    Encryption as an Impediment to Investigations, 40
    The Practical Utility of Alternatives to Exceptional Access, 45

5	OPTIONS FOR ACCESSING PLAINTEXT	49

    Options for Accessing Plaintext, 49
    Legal Tools for Obtaining Plaintext within the Current Legislative Framework, 50
        Compelled Disclosure of Biometric Identifiers or Passcodes, 50
        Compelled Assistance by Third Parties and Related Issues, 52
        Legal Aspects of Lawful Hacking, 55
    Technological Approaches for Accessing Plaintext, Limitations, and Alternatives, 56
        Approaches to Exceptional Plaintext Access, 56
        Future Cryptographic Technologies, 66
        Ways to Bypass a Plaintext Access Mandate, 67
        Alternatives to Exceptional Access, 70
    Enhanced Financial and Technical Support, 73
    Legislation Mandating Access, 76

6	INTERNATIONAL DIMENSIONS	78

    Effects of U.S. Actions on Other Countries and the International Market for U.S. Goods and Services, 80
    Global Norms, 81

7	A FRAMEWORK FOR EVALUATING APPROACHES TO ACCESS PLAINTEXT	83

APPENDIXES

A	Biographies of Committee Members	95
B	Briefers to the Committee	103

Summary

Encryption protects information stored on smartphones, laptops, and other devices—in some cases by default. Encrypted communications are provided by widely used computing devices and services—such as smartphones, laptops, and messaging applications—that are used by hundreds of millions of users. Individuals, organizations, and governments rely on encryption to counter threats from a wide range of actors, including unsophisticated and sophisticated criminals, foreign intelligence agencies, and repressive governments. Encryption on its own does not solve the challenge of providing effective security for data and systems, but it is an important tool.

At the same time, encryption is relied on by criminals to avoid investigation and prosecution, including criminals who may unknowingly benefit from default settings as well as those who deliberately use encryption. Thus, encryption complicates law enforcement and intelligence investigations. When communications are encrypted "end to end," intercepted messages cannot be understood. When a smartphone is locked and encrypted, the contents cannot be read if the phone is seized by investigators.

Yet even while the use of encryption is increasing, so is the amount of unencrypted stored data and communications and metadata. This is a result of the growth in the use of smartphones, social networks, text messaging, and other computing and electronic communications over the past decade. The result of the rise in both the amount of data and the use of encryption is that as the amount of data increases rapidly, there is both more data than ever of relevance to investigations and more data than ever that is inaccessible to investigators.

With increasing use of encryption, often by default, law enforcement and some intelligence officials have increasingly called for a reliable and sufficiently rapid and scalable way to access plaintext—decrypted data and messages—so that they can protect the public and fulfill their public safety and national security missions. In particular, law enforcement officials point to (1) the widespread and increasing use of encryption by default in widely used products and services, (2) the myriad national security threats posed by terrorist groups and foreign rivals, (3) the increasing importance of digital evidence as human activity and crime have become increasingly digital, and (4) the limited effectiveness of alternative sources of digital evidence.

Critics have objected on a number of legal and practical grounds, arguing that regulations to ensure government access to plaintext likely would (1) be ineffective, (2) pose unacceptable risks to cybersecurity, (3) pose unacceptable risks to privacy and civil liberties, (4) disadvantage U.S. providers of products and services, and (5) hamper innovation in encryption technologies. In addition, critics argue that mandating means for ensuring government access to plaintext may be less necessary in light of the wider availability of data—and especially metadata—generally, and the alternative means currently available for government officials to obtain access to encrypted data.

There are a wide variety of legal and technical options available to governments that seek access to plaintext for law enforcement and intelligence investigations. These include the following:

- Take no legislative action to regulate the use of encryption,
- Provide law enforcement with additional resources to access plaintext,
- Enact legislation that requires that device vendors or service providers provide government access to plaintext without specifying the technical means of doing so, and
- Enact legislation requiring a particular technical approach.

These are discussed in detail in Chapter 5.

Some computer scientists have reacted with concern to renewed proposals to regulate the use of encryption, citing the security risks. Several attempts have also been made in recent years to develop technical mechanisms to provide the government with exceptional access to encrypted data on locked devices and to encrypted communications that would minimize these risks. Three were presented to the Committee on Law Enforcement and Intelligence Access to Plaintext Information during its work (Box 5.1). The committee was not charged with reviewing specific proposals, but it did use these specific proposals to help develop and test its framework for evaluating suggested approaches.

The committee offers a framework (in the form of a set of questions) to ask about any path forward on encryption policy. The objective of this framework is not only to help policymakers determine whether a particular approach is optimal or desirable, but also to help ensure that any approach that policymakers might pursue is implemented in a way that maximizes its effectiveness while minimizing harmful side effects. The questions are as follows:

1. To what extent will the proposed approach be effective in permitting law enforcement and/or the intelligence community to access plaintext at or near the scale, timeliness, and reliability that proponents seek?

2. To what extent will the proposed approach affect the security of the type of data or device to which access would be required, as well as cybersecurity more broadly?

3. To what extent will the proposed approach affect the privacy, civil liberties, and human rights of targeted individuals and others?

4. To what extent will the proposed approach affect commerce, economic competitiveness, and innovation?

5. To what extent will financial costs be imposed by the proposed approach, and who will bear them?

6. To what extent is the proposed approach consistent with existing law and other government priorities?

7. To what extent will the international context affect the proposed approach, and what will be the impact of the proposed approach internationally?

8. To what extent will the proposed approach be subject to effective ongoing evaluation and oversight?

In addressing these questions, policymakers will have to contend with incomplete data about the impact of encryption on investigations as well as incomplete data about the deliberate use of encryption by criminals. It is also difficult to quantify key factors such as the additional security risks of adding exceptional access to encryption systems. There are also a number of cases where one can only speculate about future behaviors that have bearing on the implications of government regulation of encryption. These include the fraction of criminals that would use noncompliant, unbreakable encryption if the government were to require vendors to provide exceptional access and the fraction of foreign customers that would eschew U.S. products if exceptional access were required.

Policymakers will also have to contend with the trade-offs associated with encryption and government access that underlie these questions. One of the fundamental trade-offs is that adding an exceptional access capability to encryption schemes necessarily weakens their security to some degree, while the absence of an exceptional access mechanism necessarily hampers government investigations to some degree. How much security is reduced and whether the resulting level of security remains acceptable depend on the specific technical and operational details of the exceptional access mechanism and on the requirements and perspectives of users. The impact on society when an investigation is hindered or thwarted will depend on the scope and scale of the associated crime or national security threat.

There are no easy answers to and many uncertainties in responding to these questions. However, developing and debating answers to these questions will help illuminate the underlying issues and trade-offs and help inform the debate over government access to plaintext.

1

Introduction

Until the Internet era, the use of encryption was confined to sensitive government and commercial communications. With the growth of the Internet, encryption came into much wider use to protect credit card and other online transactional information. Only in the past decade, however, has encryption been widely used for ordinary communications and stored data. As laptops and smartphones developed the potential to contain large amounts of sensitive information and grew in popularity, and as states adopted data breach notification laws[1] that provided a safe harbor in cases where lost personal data had been encrypted, full-disk encryption was introduced. The use of such technologies increased after criminals began using the information stolen from individuals' devices as a way to commit fraud.

The wider deployment of encryption mechanisms used with encryption keys that are held only by users has altered the calculation for governments that seek access to encrypted communications. Previously, law enforcement and intelligence agencies were able to rely on court orders and subpoenas to providers (third parties) to seek access to communications directly from providers. However, where providers do not hold encryption keys, this access path is no longer available to the government. This trend toward deployment of encryption under end-user control was

---

[1] National Conference of State Legislatures, 2017, "Security Breach Notification Laws," April 12, http://www.ncsl.org/research/telecommunications-and-information-technology/security-breach-notification-laws.aspx.

further fueled by the growing concern about government surveillance following disclosures by Edward Snowden about U.S. surveillance programs. Vendors reacted quickly to expand encryption of data and communications by default to help distance themselves from those government programs.

Today, encryption protects information stored on or in transit between smartphones, laptops, and other devices and information stored on enterprise servers and in the cloud. Encryption is relied on to protect the data and computer systems of individuals and organizations from criminals and repressive governments. The public's use of encryption can prevent crimes such as the theft of information, thus helping make society more secure and safe. Encryption is also used by individuals, nonstate actors, and governments—including that of the United States—to prevent collection of information by government intelligence agencies. Finally, encryption enables various types of economic activity that would otherwise not be possible. Looking ahead, encryption will be important for applications that involve analyzing large volumes of shared, sensitive data.

Encrypted communications are built in to major computing platforms at both the hardware and software levels and into an array of widely used messaging applications. Absent government controls, increased integration and enhanced usability of encryption seems like a foregone conclusion. In some cases, encryption is included and enabled by default. When encryption capabilities are introduced into a major platform or widely used application, they can very rapidly end up being used by many hundreds of millions of users.

Encryption is also relied on by criminals to avoid investigation and prosecution, including criminals who may benefit from default settings as well as those who deliberately use encryption. One consequence of this widespread use is that encryption is increasingly identified as an impediment to investigations by law enforcement and to foreign intelligence information collection by U.S. intelligence agencies (see the section "Encryption as an Impediment to Investigations" in Chapter 4).

Encryption is not the only technical barrier that government investigators face when seeking access to plaintext. Even when investigators do not encounter encryption, they may confront other technical barriers. Plaintext and metadata cannot be accessed without an understanding of the multiple protocols, formats, and compression algorithms used by the software applications that transmit and store the information, elements that are not always well documented and that are subject to frequent change. This may also hamper investigations, especially if the investigating agency does not have robust technical capabilities or the cooperation of the vendor or service provider.

The U.S. government has long placed export restrictions[2] on products incorporating encryption. In the early 1990s, U.S. government agencies strongly pressed for the deposit of encryption keys with government agencies or specified third parties, a proposal that was ultimately abandoned after an extended debate over a number of issues, including the importance of spreading encryption, the technical challenges in providing for key recovery, and whether the proposal would ultimately be accepted by Congress and the public. With the increased need for encryption to secure electronic commercial data and concerns about the impact on the global competitiveness of U.S. industry, export restrictions on cryptography were relaxed in the late 1990s, ultimately paving the way for broader use of encryption in products sold domestically as well as internationally.[3]

More recently, prominent members of the law enforcement community have said that encryption is restricting access to stored data or message plaintext, even when they have a court order authorizing access. Notably, law enforcement reports a growing number of smartphones encountered during investigations that they cannot unlock (see the section "Encryption as an Impediment to Investigations" in Chapter 4). They argue that even as the volume of digital information expands, important parts of the digital world are "going dark" as more stored data and communications are encrypted by default and as information relevant to investigations is increasingly in digital form. In a 2014 speech, Federal Bureau of Investigation (FBI) Director James Comey described the broad challenge of new technology including encryption by default facing law enforcement:

> Those charged with protecting our people aren't always able to access the evidence we need to prosecute crime and prevent terrorism even with lawful authority. We have the legal authority to intercept and access communications and information pursuant to court order, but we often lack the technical ability to do so.[4]

---

[2] Nonmilitary cryptography exports from the United States are controlled by the Department of Commerce. The current regulations are complex but, generally speaking, require registration, notification, or review for products using encryption exceeding specified key lengths and require a license for export to certain countries.

[3] The export regulations, which were intended to keep sensitive technologies out of the hands of foreign adversaries, also had the side-effect of making things more complicated for U.S. vendors who preferred to sell a single version worldwide or to have as few different versions as possible, and make it more complicated for U.S. end users to acquire domestic software versions that supported a longer key length.

[4] J.B. Comey, 2014, "Going Dark: Are Technology, Privacy, and Public Safety on a Collision Course?: Remarks at the Brookings Institution, Washington, D.C.," Federal Bureau of Investigation, October 14, https://www.fbi.gov/news/speeches/going-dark-are-technology-privacy-and-public-safety-on-a-collision-course.

Since then, law enforcement officials at the federal, state, and local levels have expressed the need for a reliable and scalable way to access plaintext. Some members of the U.S. intelligence community have concurred that parts of the digital world are getting "dimmer" although not necessarily "dark."

By contrast, some, including a number of former senior members of the intelligence agencies—and a few former members of law enforcement,[5] counter that the growing use of information technology and sophisticated collection and analysis capabilities has created a plethora of capabilities for conducting investigations. The gains include "location information, information about contacts and confederates, and an array of new databases that create digital dossiers about individuals' lives."[6] Moreover, a variety of technical and business pressures may make considerably more data available to law enforcement in unencrypted form than was available a decade ago. Former National Security Agency (NSA) Director Mike McConnell observed that despite the abandonment of the 1990s effort to require exceptional access, the agency's ability to collect signals intelligence is better than at any point in history.[7]

Both perspectives share a common element: as the amount of data increases rapidly, there is both more data than ever of relevance to investigations and more data than ever that is inaccessible to investigators.

Individuals and organizations have also objected to the introduction of government access mechanisms on a number of legal and practical grounds. Their primary arguments are that any regime by which providers of products and services featuring encryption are required to provide a way for ensuring government access to plaintext likely would (1) be ineffective, (2) pose unacceptable risks to cybersecurity, (3) pose unacceptable risks to privacy and civil liberties, (4) disadvantage U.S. providers of products and services, and (5) hamper innovation in encryption technologies. Some also observe that it has never been the case that obtaining a warrant would guarantee access to the evidence sought; evidence could be hidden or destroyed before a warrant is even issued or the desired information might not have been captured in the first place.

The computer science community has also reacted to renewed proposals to regulate the use of encryption. A group of experts in computer science, cryptography, and cybersecurity, many of whom had authored a

---

[5] M. McConnell, M. Chertoff, and W. Lynn, 2015, "Why the fear over ubiquitous data encryption is overblown," *Washington Post*, July 28.

[6] P. Swire, 2015, "The golden age of surveillance," *Slate*, July, http://www.slate.com/articles/technology/future_tense/2015/07/encryption_back_doors_aren_t_necessary_we_re_already_in_a_golden_age_of.html.

[7] E. Nakashima, 2015, "Former national security officials urge government to embrace rise of encryption," *Washington Post*, December 15.

1997 study on this topic, issued a report in 2015 that concluded the following: "the damage that could be caused by law enforcement exceptional access requirements would be even greater today than it would have been 20 years ago," "new law enforcement requirements are likely to introduce unanticipated, hard to detect security flaws," and "any proposals that alter the security dynamics online should be approached with caution."[8] At the same time, some members in the technical community have begun exploring possible technical approaches to meeting government exceptional access requirements for communications and data stored on devices and seeking ways to reduce the security risks of schemes that provide exceptional access. Box 5.1 provides some examples. Box 1.1 provides examples of the diverse interests and perspectives in the encryption debate.

This report reviews how encryption is used and its applications in cybersecurity (Chapter 2), its role in protecting privacy and civil liberties (Chapter 3), the needs of law enforcement and the intelligence community for information (Chapter 4), options for accessing plaintext (Chapter 5), and the international landscape (Chapter 6). Chapter 7 provides a framework for evaluating policy or technical approaches for access to plaintext. The following sections of Chapter 1, by way of introduction to the report, briefly (1) summarize options for providing access to plaintext and possible alternative sources of information, (2) discuss the different contexts in which access could be required, and (3) provide examples of technical approaches of the sort to which the framework could be applied. Finally, the chapter previews the high-level questions in the evaluation framework that is discussed in more detail in Chapter 7.

GOVERNMENT OPTIONS

There are a wide variety of legal and technical options available to governments that seek access to plaintext for law enforcement and intelligence investigations. These can be classified[9] broadly as follows:

- *Take no legislative action to regulate the use of encryption.* Law enforcement and intelligence agencies would have to cope with a world in which

---

[8] H. Abelson, R. Anderson, S.M. Bellovin, J. Benaloh, M. Blaze, W. Diffie, J. Gilmore, et al., 2015, "Keys under doormats: Mandating insecurity by requiring government access to all data and communications," *Journal of Cybersecurity* 1(1):69-79.

[9] There are a variety of useful taxonomies. For example, a scheme developed by Kerr and Schneier describes "six kinds of workarounds: find the key, guess the key, compel the key, exploit a flaw in the encryption software, access plaintext while the device is in use, and locate another plaintext copy." See O.S. Kerr and B. Schneier, 2017, "Encryption Workarounds," GWU Law School Public Law Research Paper No. 2017-22, GWU Legal Studies Research Paper No. 2017-22, available at SSRN, https://ssrn.com/abstract=2938033.

> **BOX 1.1**
> **Interests and Perspectives in the Encryption Debate**
>
> - Protecting individuals, communities, organizations, governments, and companies who rely on encryption to safeguard their information and computer systems from hostile parties including criminal and state actors and helping society reduce the volume and impact of cyber-enabled crimes.
> - Protecting the civil liberties and human rights, including privacy, due process, and free expression and association rights of people who use computing and communications technology.
> - Protecting government, business, and private travelers, who rely on encryption to protect their mobile devices from intrusion when traveling in other countries.
> - Protecting the market share of U.S. vendors in countries whose governments or citizens are suspicious of the U.S. government.
> - Protecting public safety where access to encrypted communications or data on encrypted devices or files is sought to investigate and prosecute crimes and disrupt ongoing criminal or terrorist activity.
> - Protecting national security where access to encrypted communications or data on encrypted devices is sought for foreign intelligence collection.
> - Protecting continued innovation in encryption technologies and applications.

communications are encrypted, and devices and the data stored on them, are inaccessible. At the same time, some content would remain available where applications and business models require access to plaintext. The universe of information for potential use in investigations will likely also continue to expand, and new forms of content and metadata may become available. In addition, there are specific actions that could be taken within the current legal framework governing the use of encryption, including the following:

— Train law enforcement to employ tactics likely to mitigate the impact of encryption, such as seizing a phone while it is unlocked or surveilling a target to observe a passcode. These techniques can be used in some cases to obtain access.

— Pursue law enforcement and legal options to obtain or compel the cooperation of the investigation targets. Some options, such as compelling a target to provide a biometric to unlock a phone are currently the subject of ongoing litigation in the United States.

- *Provide additional resources to access plaintext.* The technological capabilities of U.S. law enforcement have not kept up with the rapid changes in technology. The U.S. government could provide additional resources for law enforcement and/or intelligence agencies to improve their capabilities for accessing and using digital information. These resources could be used to develop tools and train personnel to enable better use of the unencrypted digital information that is available to law enforcement and for "lawful hacking" to obtain plaintext in some circumstances by obtaining legal authorization and breaching controls on access at the points information is transmitted, received, stored, or processed. In addition, governments could invest in research and development on new ways of providing access to plaintext that may raise fewer objections—even if they provide more limited access to plaintext. This option could, of course, be pursued regardless of whether other legislative action is taken.

- *Enact legislation that requires that device vendors or service providers provide government access to plaintext without specifying the technical means of doing so.* The government could enact legislation defining an objective for accessing plaintext; the mandate could be described in a variety of ways depending on different types of problems. For example, a mandate might require that vendors be able to comply with warrants seeking access to the plaintext of the information their products and services are used to encrypt but leave it to industry to design the technical solution.
- *Enact legislation requiring a particular technical approach.* The government could enact legislation requiring a particular technical approach or regulation to select a technical approach. For example, a law or regulation could require the vendor to implement hardware-based device-level key escrow for access to stored data or require vendor or third-party key escrow for access to communications.

There are also potential options that do not involve regulation of encryption, per se, that the committee does not explore in this report because they did not seem likely to be effective or politically viable. For example, it has been proposed, by analogy to firearm sentence enhancements, that criminal penalties could be increased when encryption is used in the course of a crime. Enhanced penalties can be important if you are trying to deter the use of a particular tactic (e.g., since the use of a firearm increases the risk to public safety, stiffer penalties apply). Unlike guns, however, which the criminal must affirmatively decide to use when committing an offense, encryption is widely embedded in commercial products and services, is often enabled by default, and may not even be in the direct control of the end user. Put another way, a criminal would have to affirmatively decide to avoid encryption to reduce the risk of an enhanced penalty, a most unlikely outcome. One could also consider making it a crime to offer encryption products for criminal purposes. However, such cases are likely already covered by existing aiding and abetting laws, and it seems easy to circumvent such statutes simply by marketing the product for another purpose.

SCOPE AND CONTEXT FOR ACCESS

Several of the options above contemplate government regulation of service providers and vendors. Such measures could be brought to bear in a variety of ways and circumstances and applied narrowly or broadly. The following are some of the relevant dimensions of this context:

- *Scope*. Regulation might be very broad, encompassing both enterprise and personal stored data and communications, or more narrow—for example, covering only access to the contents of smartphones or communications using consumer messaging applications.
- *Type of data*. Regulations might apply to encrypted data stored in devices, such as smartphones or laptops; data stored by cloud services; and/or the content of network communications.
- *Type of user*. Regulation might apply to all (or a subset of) commercial entities or private citizens. Notably, some regulated entities (e.g., banks) already have legal obligations to provide data, and enterprises need recovery methods for business continuity. By contrast, private citizens do not generally have such regulatory requirements; they may nevertheless opt for a capability to recover their data. The situation is blurred when people use personal devices in business settings and further complicated because the same devices and services are often used in both personal and business settings.
- *Application layer*. Regulations might apply only to encryption provided by a device's operating system, which would provide access to information not otherwise encrypted, but they would not enable access to data separately encrypted by individual applications. Alternatively, regulations might be applied to applications that run on a device or the services to which the applications connect.
- *Different crimes or intelligence priorities*. For example, individuals might be compelled to reveal a passcode only if needed for the investigation of serious crimes, which could be argued to limit the impact on civil liberties.

EVALUATION FRAMEWORK

Chapter 7 provides an evaluation framework in the form of questions that the committee believes must be addressed in any proposal to provide government access to plaintext. The objective of this framework is not only to help policymakers determine whether a particular approach is optimal or desirable, but also to help ensure that any approach that policymakers might pursue is implemented in a way that maximizes its effectiveness while minimizing harmful side effects. The questions are as follows:

1. To what extent will the proposed approach be effective in permitting law enforcement and/or the intelligence community to access plaintext at or near the scale, timeliness, and reliability that proponents seek?
2. To what extent will the proposed approach affect the security of the type of data or device to which access would be required, as well as cybersecurity more broadly?
3. To what extent will the proposed approach affect the privacy, civil liberties, and human rights of targeted individuals and others?
4. To what extent will the proposed approach affect commerce, economic competitiveness, and innovation?
5. To what extent will financial costs be imposed by the proposed approach, and who will bear them?
6. To what extent is the proposed approach consistent with existing law and other government priorities?
7. To what extent will the international context affect the proposed approach, and what will be the impact of the proposed approach internationally?
8. To what extent will the proposed approach be subject to effective ongoing evaluation and oversight?

The reader may find it helpful to keep these questions in mind when reading the examples and analysis in subsequent chapters of this report.

2

Encryption and Its Applications

For most of recorded history, encryption has been used to protect the secrecy of communications between a sender and a receiver. Governments have historically been heavy users of encryption. The Caesar cipher goes back to the Roman Empire. Ciphers were used by both sides in the American Revolutionary War. Histories of World War II dwell at length on the contribution of defeating German and Japanese encryption systems to the Allied victory. At the same time, the Allies also relied on encryption systems, some of which were defeated by Axis codebreakers. Governments' reliance on encrypted communications continues to the present day.

In recent years, encryption has become far more widely available on a wide range of consumer and business products and services. Increasingly, encryption is available by default—often without the user even being aware of it—and the keys for decrypting data are held by individual users. As a result, more data is routinely encrypted today than ever before.

Today, encryption protects the communications of individuals and organizations from unsophisticated and sophisticated criminals and repressive governments. It assures the security of electronic commerce transactions over the Internet—for example making it possible to transmit credit card numbers. It protects information stored on smartphones, laptops, and other devices. Encrypted communication capabilities are built into major computing platforms and in an array of messaging applications that are used by hundreds of millions of users.

Computer and communications systems use cryptography for three broad purposes—to protect the confidentiality of information (i.e., encryption), to protect the integrity of information, and to authenticate the originator or sender of information. Applications that require the secrecy of large volumes of information use symmetric cryptography. Asymmetric (public key) cryptography is frequently used to securely disseminate keys that are used in symmetric cryptography. For example, cryptography enables the secure distribution of regular software updates, including security patches, over a network and is used to verify the identity of individuals and organizations. This report focuses largely on the first application, encryption protecting confidentiality. However, it touches on another use of cryptography: schemes to provide exceptional access to information stored on smartphones or laptops that are locked with a passcode may involve modifications to the cryptography that implements the locking mechanism.

The increased availability and use of encryption—most notably to protect access to data stored on smartphones and to keep Internet messages confidential—means that it is increasingly encountered in investigations by law enforcement and intelligence agencies.[1]

This chapter provides a basic introduction to encryption and its uses. It provides context for subsequent discussions of mechanisms that would afford government access and associated technical and operational risks. It begins with a description of the different kinds of encryption that are important today and with an overview of the ways that encryption systems are created. It then provides an overview of some of the ways that modern computer and communications systems use encryption to provide a secure experience to their end users. This is followed by a description of the issues and challenges of managing the cryptographic keys that encryption systems rely on. The chapter concludes with a discussion of the threats that modern encryption systems face and attempt to defeat.

WHAT IS ENCRYPTION?

Encryption schemes transform a plaintext message (or stored data) into a ciphertext in such a way that the ciphertext reveals little or no information about the original plaintext. Encryption schemes have the following three components: a key generation algorithm, an encryption algorithm, and a decryption algorithm. The encryption algorithm takes plaintext and an encryption key as input and returns a ciphertext. The decryption algorithm takes as input a ciphertext and a decryption key and returns the plaintext.

---

[1] See the section "Encryption as an Impediment to Investigations" in Chapter 4 for a discussion of data on how often encryption is encountered in investigations and its impacts.

In a symmetric scheme, the encryption and decryption keys are the same and must be kept secret. Without the secret key, there is no practical way to decrypt the data.

One can visualize the symmetric encryption process as putting plaintext data in a box and then locking the box using a secret key. The box can be opened only using the same secret key. Provided that one uses a suitable algorithm, a properly engineered implementation, and a sufficiently long key, the encryption is unbreakable (Box 2.1).

A physical box can be forced open with tools. By contrast, breaking encryption requires trying each possible key until the correct one is found; this can take an extremely long time. Knowing (including guessing or stealing) the key is the only practical way to retrieve the data unless one can circumvent the encryption by obtaining the information before it is encrypted or after it is decrypted (unless a flaw in the encryption software or cryptographic algorithm can be found and exploited).

In an asymmetric or public-key encryption scheme, the encryption and decryption keys are different, and only the decryption key must be kept secret. The encryptor uses one key, called a public key, while the decryptor uses a different key, called a private key. As the name suggests, the public key is public and enables anyone to encrypt messages. Only the corresponding private key can decrypt the resulting ciphertexts.

One can visualize the public-key encryption process as placing the data in a box that locks as soon as one closes the lid. Anyone can create such a box and lock it, but only someone in possession of the secret key can unlock the box. As with symmetric encryption, knowing the key is the only practical way to retrieve the data, unless one can steal the key or obtain the information before it is encrypted or after it is decrypted.

Under some circumstances, encryption schemes may provide for authorized third-party access to encrypted information. Following a 1996 National Research Council report on encryption, this report uses the phrase exceptional access to

> Stress that the situation is not one that was included within the intended bounds of the original transaction, but is an unusual subsequent event. Exceptional access refers to situations in which an authorized party needs and can obtain the plaintext of encrypted data (for storage or communications). The word "exceptional" is used in contrast to the word "routine" and connotes something unusual about the circumstances under which access is required. Government exceptional access refers to the case in which government has a need for access to information under specific circumstances authorized by law.[2]

---

[2] National Research Council, 1996, *Cryptography's Role in Securing the Information Society*, National Academy Press, Washington, D.C., p. 80.

BOX 2.1
How Strong Is "Strong?"
Defining Encryption for This Report

The term "strong encryption" sometimes arises in the context of the policy debate around government access to plaintext. Its use goes back to the days when the U.S. government limited the wide availability of some encryption products by setting a limit on the key size of exportable algorithms. In those days, strong encryption algorithms were those that exceeded the government limit by a reasonable margin (40 bit exportable; 56 bit strong).

Today, it is used more generally to denote an encryption scheme with one or more of the properties that make it especially difficult for a well-resourced attacker to defeat it. Sometimes, "strong encryption" is used in the current debate simply as a short-hand for encryption that it is not affordable or practicable for government investigators to defeat, at least not at scale.

The properties that make a scheme difficult to defeat include an appropriate choice of cryptographic algorithms and protocols, a well-engineered implementation, use of sufficiently long key lengths, and the absence of deliberately introduced hidden flaws. Some use the term for encryption schemes that do not provide technical mechanisms for government exceptional access, while others would consider schemes that include properly engineered access mechanisms to be "strong."

Given the different view on what it means for encryption to be "strong" and given the existence of widely accepted standards for encryption technology, this report eschews the term "strong." Unless otherwise qualified, when this report uses the term "encryption," it means encrypting data in a way that makes it impractically difficult for unauthorized individuals to gain access to plaintext. Today, this level of difficulty corresponds to the use of encryption that follows the latest recommendations of the European Union Agency for Network and Information Security,[1] the National Institute of Standards and Technology,[2] or the National Security Agency.[3]

---

[1] European Union Agency for Network and Information Security, 2014, *Algorithms, Key Size and Parameters Report 2014*, November 21, https://www.enisa.europa.eu/publications/algorithms-key-size-and-parameters-report-2014.

[2] E. Barker, 2016, *Recommendation for Key Management: Part 1*, General NIST Special Publication 800-57, Part 1 Revision 4, National Institute of Standards and Technology, U.S. Department of Commerce, January, http://nvlpubs.nist.gov/nistpubs/SpecialPublications/NIST.SP.800-57pt1r4.pdf.

[3] National Security Agency, 2015, *Commercial National Security Algorithm Suite*, August 19, https://www.iad.gov/iad/programs/iad-initiatives/cnsa-suite.cfm.

Exceptional access also applies in a business context, where an employer can access information encrypted by an employee, and in an end-user context, such as data recovery after an encryption key is lost.

DESIGNING ENCRYPTION

The design and standardization of secure encryption algorithms is a challenging task. Although there are encryption algorithms that are perfectly secure in the sense that they are unbreakable,[3] these schemes are rarely deployed in the real world because they are not practical. Even though the encryption schemes that are deployed in practice are not perfectly secure, their security is supported by a rigorous design process backed by a mathematically sound framework that allows cryptographers to carefully study and analyze their strengths and weaknesses.

The process of reviewing and assessing the security of symmetric encryption schemes with the aim of endorsing a scheme as a standard for broad use in the United States and in much of the world generally occurs through a world-wide competition to which experts in symmetric encryption submit their designs. The algorithms are then cryptanalyzed (i.e., experts study their properties and attempt to defeat them) for years, and the most resilient one is chosen. For example, the widely used Advanced Encryption Standard (AES) and Secure Hash Algorithm-3 (SHA-3) cryptographic standards were evaluated and standardized through competitions organized by the National Institute of Standards and Technology (NIST).[4] In the end, confidence in the security of these encryption schemes relies in part on their design and in part on the fact that they withstood years of cryptanalytic effort. Wide adoption of resulting algorithms, such as occurred with AES, results in increased security for all.

Encryption and other security functions are performed by cryptographic protocols, which describe how cryptographic algorithms are used to perform the tasks necessary to carry out that function. For example, a protocol for confidential communications must describe how a sender and receiver authenticate each other, how they agree on or establish encryption keys, and how the messages they exchange are encrypted and transported across the network.

The challenge of designing practical and secure encryption is magnified by the fact that encryption algorithms and protocols are notoriously fragile. Even a small and seemingly innocuous change in their design

---

[3] One-time pad encryption cannot be broken but requires that a random and unique key as long as the message be generated and shared with the receiver.

[4] Country-specific cryptography, such as that developed for use in China and Russia, does not follow such an open process.

can break them completely.[5] Moreover, bugs in the software that implements the algorithms can go undetected for years.[6] If a new encryption scheme were to be developed for the purpose of supporting third-party access, it would require similar attention to design and engineering and a comparable amount of scrutiny if it were to be trusted as much as current schemes.[7]

Cryptography is a very active research field in which new techniques continue to be developed, standardized, and deployed. For example, the most widely used symmetric encryption method, AES, was standardized in the year 2001. A common way to use AES, called AES-Galois/Counter Mode, was developed in 2005. A new method for encrypting credit card data, called format-preserving encryption, was standardized in 2013. Public-key ciphers designed to withstand quantum computers (which—if realized at large scale—would provide powerful new capabilities to attackers seeking to break encryption) are only now being developed and are expected to be standardized in the mid-2020s.[8] Since 2008, new encryption methods have been invented that enable encrypted data to be processed without decryption. Such techniques—if their performance can be improved so that they are practical—could reduce, for example, the risk of using cloud computing to process confidential data and would also have implications for government access. One potential consequence of this continuing innovation to consider is whether government policies requiring the use of particular technologies may impede future advances. For example, innovation in the United States might well be inhibited if only a single method of encryption or class of encryption methods were allowed domestically.

---

[5] For example, the addition of a compression feature for Transport Layer Security (TLS) packets introduced a significant vulnerability by opening up a powerful side-channel attack. See J. Kelsey, 2002, "Compression and information leakage of plaintext," pp. 263-276 in *Revised Papers from the 9th International Workshop on Fast Software Encryption, FSE '02*, Springer-Verlag, London, U.K., http://dl.acm.org/citation.cfm?id=647937.741226. This vulnerability is the basis of the Compression Ratio Info-leak Made Easy (CRIME) exploit against secret Web cookies over connections that use data compression, allowing an attacker to hijack an authenticated session.

[6] For example, a study of encryption keys used for Web traffic revealed vulnerabilities from poorly implemented key-generation algorithms. See A. Lenstra, J.P. Hughes, M. Augier, J.W. Bos, T. Kleinjung, and C. Wachter, 2012, "Ron was wrong, Whit is right," *IACR Technical Report*, https://eprint.iacr.org/2012/064.pdf.

[7] This point was made in a 1996 National Research Council report, but the recommendation to implement and test an exceptional access system at scale was never carried out. See National Research Council, 1996, *Cryptography's Role in Securing the Information Society*, National Academy Press, Washington, D.C.

[8] National Institute of Standards and Technology, 2017, "Post-Quantum Crypto Project: Workshops/Timeline," April 24, http://csrc.nist.gov/groups/ST/post-quantum-crypto/workshops.html.

Real-world systems use a multitude of keys for many different purposes. Some are used to encrypt messages, some are used to encrypt other keys, and others are used to authenticate messages or users. Most often, encryption is used in the design of secure systems as a way to reduce the amount of information that needs protecting by other means. By encrypting data, it is possible to render components of a system incapable of compromising the data they process, thus reducing the portion of the system that requires deep security analysis.

It is critical to properly manage and secure keys. They must be securely created, stored, distributed, certified, backed up, updated, revoked, and deleted. Keys often have a finite lifetime, determined by their specific usage and their risk of exposure. For example, keys used to encrypt messages that are only retained for a short period of time ("ephemeral" messages) tend to have brief lifetimes. Other keys that are used to generate other keys tend to have longer lifetimes (often many years) and require especially strong protection. It is a best practice to delete all copies of a key when it is no longer needed.

APPLICATIONS OF ENCRYPTION

Computer applications, software, and hardware all integrate encryption to accomplish objectives that users value. A single laptop or smartphone today, for instance, commonly deploys encryption in multiple different ways, including in the hardware, the firmware that connects the hardware and the operating system, and a large portion of the software that runs on the device. The pervasiveness of encryption is relevant to public debates about exceptional access, because only certain uses of cryptography in a laptop or smartphone enable encryption of users' data of potential interest to law enforcement or intelligence agencies. Thus a mandate for exceptional access would have to be targeted to specific uses of cryptography where the specifics vary according to the device. This section provides some highly simplified examples of some of these applications and the ways that they depend on encryption; the focus is on giving a sense of the role of encryption rather than full details of its implementation.

Protecting Stored Files

Applications that protect a single file or a few files almost always use symmetric encryption to protect the file content. The key for the symmetric encryption system may be entered into the program by the user, derived from a user-supplied password, entered from a hardware token, protected by an asymmetric encryption system in which the symmetric encryption key is encrypted under a public key and decrypted when the corresponding private key is provided, or some combination of these. For example, in the Encrypting File System that is integrated into Microsoft Windows, the user's private key is decrypted by the operating system when the user logs in.

A related use of encryption is to functionally "erase" data. If data is encrypted and the key is destroyed, the data becomes inaccessible as if it were erased. In fact, deleting the key is even better than deleting the data because deleting the key renders all copies of the data inaccessible (even backups) and obviates the need to wipe storage media.

Full Disk Encryption

Many modern operating systems support full disk[9] encryption, which protects both user data and system programs from disclosure. As with the file encryption scenario outlined above, the files themselves are protected using symmetric encryption. Additional protective measures combining operating system software and computer hardware protect the system files from modification (so that modified program files cannot, for example, access encrypted data and transfer it to an unauthorized user once it has been decrypted).

Full disk encryption systems are complex. The underlying hardware or firmware must include a mechanism that verifies a digital signature on the first firmware and software components to run after the system is booted, thus ensuring that they have not been maliciously modified. After this validation has been completed, and after the user has authenticated to the system with a passcode, token, or both, the hardware provides access to a secret (asymmetric) key that the software then uses to decrypt a stored symmetric key that is in turn used to decrypt the contents of the disk.

Full disk encryption systems must meet a variety of real-world requirements. It must be possible to securely update signed firmware and software components in case errors are found. It must also be possible to change user passcodes—ideally without having to decrypt and re-encrypt the entire content of the disk. Full disk encryption systems are usually configured so the secret key protecting the disk encryption key is erased (and the decrypted contents of disk made unavailable) if too many invalid passcodes are entered (see the next section). If a mechanism for entering a recovery key (which should be physically protected in a physically separate location) is provided, it allows users to regain access

---

[9] In this report "disk" is used to include the solid-state drives implemented with flash memory chips that are used as mass storage in smartphones and many laptops.

to their data in the event the key erasure feature is triggered or if a major hardware or software failure occurs. Meeting each of these requirements adds complexity to the full disk encryption system.[10]

Device Locking

Mobile devices and the data they contain are frequently protected by locking[11] mechanisms that ensure, by default, that phone data is encrypted whenever the screen is locked and that only the user can unlock the phone and its contents. For phones, this combination of cryptographic passcode protection and full disk encryption was introduced as the default setting in Apple's iOS 9 and Android's Marshmallow system, although not all vendors of Android phones implement this encryption.[12]

The key needed to unlock the phone is a combination of the user's passcode and the phone's hardware key. Each time an incorrect passcode is entered, the phone delays the next attempt. After a limited number of incorrect attempts, the key is erased, making the data inaccessible. Users can also configure their phones to use a biometric, such as a fingerprint or face, instead of a passcode; after a limited number of failed recognition attempts or a limited period of time, the phone reverts to the passcode unlock mechanism. These measures deter phone theft and protect users' data but also can make it extremely difficult for law enforcement to access data that may be relevant to an investigation if the data is stored only on the locked device.

Virtual Private Networks

A virtual private network (VPN) is a way of creating an encrypted connection between a remote user and a site. By enabling remote users to seamlessly connect to the organization's networks, VPNs provide a convenient way for organizations to operate across multiple locations. Thus a traveling employee can safely access his or her work network from a hotel room anywhere in the world. VPNs operate by using symmetric cryptography to encrypt packets of data to be transmitted between central and remote locations, and then embedding the encrypted packets in "outer" packets that are routed over the Internet. The encrypted packets include

---

[10] In fact, the description provided here is simplified with respect to the number and relationships of the cryptographic keys and validations actually required.

[11] "Locking" has been used in various ways with respect to phones. Here "locking" simply means that users must enter a passcode or otherwise authenticate themselves before the device will function.

[12] Apple provides updates for all iPhones. Although Google develops the Android operating system, updates are handled by the manufacturers that use it.

routing and other information that enables them—once decrypted—to reach their destination within the organization's network.

VPN systems include mechanisms that allow each end of the connection to authenticate to the other, either using asymmetric cryptography or symmetric cryptography with a shared key at each end of the connection. Keys may be derived from a user-entered password, from a code generated by a hardware token, or both. Authentication is important and authentication mechanisms must be designed carefully to prevent a "man in the middle" from masquerading as the "other user" to both endpoints of the communication and intercepting and decrypting all of the encrypted traffic.

Secure Web Browsing

Each time a user visits an e-commerce website or a Web-based email server[13] such as Gmail or Hotmail, he or she does so through an encrypted connection. A protocol called TLS provides the encrypted connection. It uses authentication protocols based on asymmetric cryptography and signed certificates to verify that the server is the one whose name the user typed into the browser. It then uses public key encryption to negotiate a symmetric key for the browsing session and uses that symmetric key to encrypt the session traffic. Almost all Web browsers and servers support TLS or one of its predecessors, and many web servers have the public-key certificates necessary to support encrypted sessions.

The history of the protocols used for secure Web browsing provides a compelling illustration of how difficult it is to develop encryption protocols and the care that must be taken when adding capabilities to accommodate government requirements. In the early days of the Internet, government restrictions limited the strength of symmetric encryption that could be implemented by browsers and servers sold outside the United States. Although those restrictions have been removed, to ensure backward compatibility weak encryption remains as an option (and not by default) in many products. Although the weak encryption is not typically on by default, it is possible for an attacker to force browsers and servers that implement some protocol versions to "fall back" to older and weaker

---

[13] Note that web-based email services are not the same as "e-mail encryption." Although the user's connection to the web-based email server is protected by secure browsing, the email message is available to the server in unencrypted form, in contrast to the email encryption scenario where the message is only unencrypted on the sender's and recipient's local devices.

encryption suites.[14] Additionally, TLS and its predecessors are very complex, and bugs in implementations (and in the protocols themselves for earlier versions) have resulted in widespread weaknesses.

Operators of Internet services and suppliers of browsers and servers are aware of these limitations and continue to work to eliminate them by introducing new security features, conducting continuing analyses and attempts at formal verification of the TLS protocols, and searching for and removing weaknesses.

Secure Messaging

Secure messaging applications use end-to-end encryption protocols to prevent third parties as well as the messaging service provider from having access to the plaintext of messages. The Signal protocol, designed by Open Whisper Systems, is used in several widely used messaging applications including Signal, WhatsApp, secret conversations in Facebook Messenger, the "incognito mode" of Google Allo, and Skype. When a user registers for a messaging service, the app sends a public identity key, public session set-up key, and a batch of public one-time session set-up keys to the messaging service's server and retains the corresponding set of private keys. To communicate with another user, the initiating app establishes an encrypted session. To do so, the initiator's app requests a set of public keys for the recipient from a public-key server. Both the initiator and recipient use each other's public keys to generate a master secret key for the session. Each message is then encrypted using symmetric encryption with a unique message key computed based on the master secret key. This message key is ephemeral: it cannot be reconstructed from the current session state after the message has been transmitted or received.[15] As a result of this approach, known as forward secrecy and commonly used to protect communications, it is not possible to decrypt multiple past communications by finding or breaking a single key. That is, even if encryption keys from a user's smartphone are compromised, they cannot be used to go back in time to decrypt previously transmitted messages.

---

[14] B. Beurdouche, K. Bhargavan, A. Delignat-Lavaud, C. Fournet, M. Kohlweiss, A. Pironti, P.-Y. Strub, and J.K. Zinzindohoue 2015, "A messy state of the union: Taming the composite state machines of TLS," pp. 535-552 in *2015 IEEE Symposium on Security and Privacy*, doi:10.1109/SP.2015.39.

[15] WhatsApp, 2017, "WhatsApp Encryption Overview," July 6, https://www.whatsapp.com/security/WhatsApp-Security-Whitepaper.pdf.

Protecting Confidentiality in Cloud or Third-Party Computing

Cloud computing and storage are changing how organizations use and manage their data and, of particular relevance here, the data of their customers. Familiar examples of consumer services that store data in the cloud include e-mail services such as Google's Gmail and file storage and sharing services such as Dropbox. Cloud services are also used to back up and restore data on smartphones or laptops. Encryption is generally used to protect the confidentiality of that data. Depending on how the service is architected and the business model of the service provider, the provider may or may not have access to the keys needed to decrypt the data.

New and emerging techniques enable better protection of this data and will complicate future efforts by investigators to access data in some situations. For example, one indication of future technology trends toward greater protection of data in the cloud can be seen in the growing trend of cloud providers to support virtual machines where encrypted data is decrypted only at the time the data is actually used.[16] In the long term, emerging techniques for computing on data without decrypting it, such as homomorphic encryption, will further protect data in the cloud and complicate efforts to access it. Because these techniques are likely to be more costly to use than other forms of encryption, it is expected that they will be used—if and when they are adopted—with especially sensitive types of data such as medical information.

ENCRYPTION AND THE EXPANDING CYBER THREAT

The United States faces a significant and growing cybersecurity threat. Indeed, it has topped the list of global threats in the *Worldwide Threat Assessment of the US Intelligence Community* since 2013. The 2017 threat assessment states:

> Cyber threats are already challenging public trust and confidence in global institutions, governance, and norms, while imposing costs on the US and global economies. Cyber threats also pose an increasing risk to public health, safety, and prosperity as cyber technologies are integrated with critical infrastructure in key sectors.[17]

---

[16] This service uses new cryptography and trusted execution technologies that have been added to microprocessors. See Microsoft Corporation, 2017, "(Cloud) Tip of the Day: Introducing Azure confidential computing," October 3, https://blogs.technet.microsoft.com/tip_of_the_day/2017/10/03/cloud-tip-of-the-day-introducing-azure-confidential-computing/.

[17] Office of the Director of National Intelligence, 2017, "Statement for the Record: Worldwide Threat Assessment of the US Intelligence Community," May 11, https://www.dni.gov/files/documents/Newsroom/Testimonies/SSCI%20Unclassified%20SFR%20-%20Final.pdf.

As more than a decade of high-profile attacks has shown, it is proving increasingly difficult to secure data or the computerized systems that control the nation's financial services, communications, health care, elections, utilities, factories, supply chains, and transportation sectors. Attacks are being made against individuals, governments, universities, research organizations, and civil society groups. As digital infrastructure becomes more pervasive and interconnected, both its accessibility to attackers around the world and the consequences of successful attacks are growing. The threat environment continues to worsen, as evidenced by the attacks described below. In many cases, encryption is an important—and sometimes necessary—tool in responding to this challenge.

In considering the role of encryption in combating cyber threats, one important consideration is when and how much encryption can help counter a threat. Not all cyber threats can necessarily be prevented by encryption; see the discussion at the end of the following section. Another important consideration is how much additional risk is introduced by exceptional access mechanisms and whether that added risk is acceptable in the context of particular applications and threats and when weighed against the benefits. The section "Technological Approaches for Accessing Plaintext, Limitations, and Alternatives" in Chapter 5 discusses several possible technical mechanisms for exceptional access and some of the associated risks.

Another important consideration is the context in which a regulation to provide government exceptional access would apply. For example, a regulation that applies to mass-market messaging applications would not directly affect the use of encryption to protect credit card numbers in e-commerce applications. On the other hand, if smartphones are used to provide authentication codes in a multifactor authentication scheme, a requirement for exceptional access to unlock smartphones adds some degree of risk that the authentication codes could be obtained from a lost or stolen phone.

Cyber Threats

Network-enabled cyber threats first appeared in the mid-1980s.[18] These were the opening wedge in what became an increasingly serious series of attacks. In the 1990s, attackers took advantage of poorly secured systems and the vulnerable security architectures in computer products, mostly to demonstrate weaknesses and gain public recognition.[19] As the use of computers and the Internet grew, attacks became increasingly sophisticated and the targets more and more valuable. Criminal hackers jumped into the trade. Another change came with state-sponsored attacks. Digitization and the growth of interconnected networks created a ripe environment for espionage.

The number of places that contain potentially sensitive information continues to grow. The "big data" revolution has resulted in a great deal more information about individuals being collected, stored, and analyzed. Consequently, data has become an increasing target and encryption and other applications of cryptography have become important—and sometimes essential—tools for protecting data.

Beginning around 2005, industry and government began encountering advanced persistent threat (APT) agents—hackers who would mount repeated attacks against the same target over a period of a number of months or longer. Often the attack came through "spear phishing" emails that appeared to originate from legitimate sources and were tailored to specific targets. These were used to fool the recipient into providing access credentials for targeted systems (such a technique was used to hack e-mail during the 2016 U.S. presidential election). Many companies and government agencies around the world—including the U.K. Parliament, Oak Ridge National Laboratory, and Northrup Grumman—have fallen prey

---

[18] An investigation over a missing 75 cents at the Lawrence Berkeley National Laboratory eventually revealed a German hacker stealing U.S. Department of Defense documents that he was selling to the KGB (C. Stoll, 2005, *The Cuckoo's Egg: Tracking a Spy through the Maze of Computer Espionage*, Simon & Schuster, New York). Several years later, in what was essentially an experiment that escaped the laboratory, the Morris Worm brought down the nascent ARPANet when an incorrect parameter caused the worm to proliferate far faster and more broadly than intended (see, e.g., H. Orman, 2003, "The Morris worm: A fifteen-year perspective," *IEEE Security and Privacy* 99(5):35-43).

[19] One example of this, there are many, is that the Melissa and ILOVEYOU viruses were in e-mail attachments but were able to access Microsoft users' address books and thus mail themselves on to new victims.

to this form of attack. Even RSA Security, a leading provider of security tools, was victimized by an APT attack.[20]

Many nations are experiencing cyber threats, but the United States is particularly threatened. In 2010, former NSA Director Mike McConnell noted, "The United States is fighting a cyber-war today, and we are losing. . . . As the most wired nation on Earth, we offer the most targets of significance, yet our cyber-defenses are woefully lacking."[21] Since then, reported intelligence attacks on the United States have been growing in severity:

- In a 2015 attack attributed to Chinese actors, hackers gained access to 80 million customer records at Anthem, the second largest health insurer in the United States.[22]
- In 2015, suspected Chinese hackers illegally accessed Office of Personnel Management computers and stole more than 21.5 million records including fingerprints of government employees and contractors holding security clearances. The stolen data included family, financial, travel, and health information about the people with access to the nation's secrets.[23]
- Russian intelligence agencies stole emails from the Democratic National Committee servers in 2015 and the account of the Democratic presidential candidate's campaign chair in 2016.[24]

Recent years have also seen the emergence of cyberattacks intended to have physical impacts, such as attacks on industrial control systems and public utilities.

Some threats have abated in recent years, while others have grown

---

[20] An attacker sent e-mails with the subject "2011 Recruitment Plan" to a number of RSA Security employees over 2 days. One employee opened the attached Excel spreadsheet, which installed malware that used a previously unknown bug—a zero-day vulnerability—in Adobe Flash software. Using this, the attacker was able to access passwords to other accounts. See RSA Fraud Action Research Labs, 2011, "Anatomy of an Attack," April 1, https://blogs.rsa.com/anatomy-of-an-attack/.

[21] M. McConnell, 2010, "Mike McConnell on how to win the cyber-war we're losing," *Washington Post* 28:B01.

[22] D. Harwell and E. Nakashima, 2015, "China suspected in major hacking of health insurer," *Washington Post*, February 5.

[23] J.H. Davis, 2015, "Hacking of government computers exposed 21.5 million people," *New York Times*, July 9.

[24] Office of the Director of National Intelligence, 2017, *A Background to "Assessing Russian Activities and Intentions in Recent US Elections": The Analytic Process and Cyber Incident Attribution*, Intelligence Community Assessment ICA 2017-01D, January 6, https://www.dni.gov/files/documents/ICA_2017_01.pdf.

more severe. Some nations, including North Korea[25] and Russia, have viewed cyberattacks as an effective way to achieve national objectives without resorting to kinetic weapons. In 2013, Russia embarked on a plan to "[fight] a war without fighting a war," and cyberattacks provided an excellent tool for doing so.[26] The activities in the 2016 U.S. presidential election are one example of this strategy.

None of the attacks listed above would have been prevented by encryption, although it may have made them more difficult to carry out. Some appear to have been conducted by using "phishing" emails to entice authorized users to give up their authentication credentials and then using the stolen credentials to gain privileges necessary to access, decrypt, and exfiltrate the targeted data. Others resulted from devices being protected only by unchanged default passwords. Several of the attacks point to the need for greater use of secure two-factor authentication. One widely used approach uses smartphones. Doing so securely depends on device locking, as described above.

Encryption can reduce the risk or consequence of attacks in several ways. It greatly reduces the risks when data is stolen or accidentally leaked or stored on a device such as a phone or laptop that is lost or stolen. It forces an adversary seeking to exfiltrate data to not only steal the device but also gain access to the keys used to encrypt it. Encryption thus forces adversaries to launch different kinds of attacks, making such attacks more difficult and costly to execute. In addition, the appropriate use of encryption may make it more difficult for an adversary to make use of the information it has taken. The next section provides details of the role of encryption in creating secure systems.

The Role of Encryption and Other Forms of Cryptography in Cybersecurity

In the face of this widespread and escalating threat, cryptography is an important tool for protecting data and systems, including reducing the volume and impact of cyber-enabled crime. Cryptography is used in a number of ways, but four are most critical.

First, encryption is used to protect stored data against disclosure. (Encryption does not protect against all threats—malware running on a phone or malware running with the privileges of authorized users of an encrypted database can see the unencrypted data.) This explains why

---

[25] North Korea obtained confidential information of Sony Pictures Entertainment, a U.S.-based company, in 2014. President Obama characterized the incident as a national security threat.

[26] C.K. Bartles, 2016, "Getting Gerasimov right," *Military Review* 96(1):30.

the majority of the 48 states that have enacted data breach notification laws do not require notification if the lost or stolen data is encrypted: modern encryption renders the data effectively meaningless provided that the encryption keys are not compromised and there are no exploitable flaws in the encryption system. The security of encrypted data also explains why vendors such as Google and Apple have moved to default device encryption on mobile phones. As long as user passwords are sufficiently strong, lost and stolen devices do not reveal the data inside them.

Second, encryption is a crucial tool for protecting data in transmission. This is critically important for online banking, purchases, contracts, and telemedicine applications, where it is important not only that the data is not intercepted, but also that it is not altered. Encryption makes it possible to protect the data being transmitted—and to create simple mathematical "seals" than can alert either the sender or receiver (or an auditor or a court) if the data has been tampered with. The increasing shift from unencrypted to encrypted Web protocols is an example of moving to Internet connections that are secure by default. Encryption can protect communications from "man in the middle attacks" and prevent intrusions into organizational networks.

Third, cryptography provides a widely used tool for authenticating individuals and institutions: Using public-key cryptography, it is possible for one party to authenticate the identity of another. A sender "Alice" creates a message digitally signed with her private key. If the receiver "Bob" is able to decrypt this message using Alice's public key, he knows that the sender possesses Alice's private key.

Fourth, cryptography used to lock devices is an important enabler of multifactor authentication that uses smartphones. Multifactor authentication, which is the best available technology for defending against phishing attacks that seek to entice a user into giving up his or her password to a spoofed website makes use of several separate pieces of evidence for authentication. In a widely used scenario, the user provides a password to the website and also verifies intent to access the site by approving an authentication request on his/her smartphone or by entering into the website a numeric code that the website sends to the smartphone. The interaction between website and smartphone may be protected using cryptography, and each authentication attempt involves unique values that can be used only once. Encryption is critical to prevent an attacker from acting as a "man in the middle" between user and/or smartphone and server, intercepting the authentication data, and capturing control of the user's session.

Another approach, which is becoming more widespread, is to use apps running on smartphones as trusted authenticators for accessing online services. Their security depends on keeping an unauthorized user from being able to unlock the smartphone and access the authenticator app. Thus, any weakness introduced into the mechanism for unlocking smartphones can increase the risk that the authentication mechanism could be compromised.

Encryption is similarly important for maintaining the security of those biometric authentication mechanisms that rely on transmitting biometric information over the network.

The Limits of Encryption for Cybersecurity

Cryptography itself is a challenging science. Furthermore, correctly implementing and properly managing encryption systems is very difficult. For example, there have been many instances where the techniques used to construct public-private key pairs have been found to have had serious flaws.[27]

Moreover, with the exception of specialized, emerging techniques for computing with encrypted data, for data to be used, it must at some point be decrypted into plaintext. At that moment, it is vulnerable to theft. Also, because encryption keys are usually long and complex, users often store them and then protect them with passwords, which are much more vulnerable because they must be something a human can remember and type.

Nonetheless encryption and other uses of cryptography remain an essential tool for enhancing cybersecurity against escalating cyber threats. They are critical parts of a system that includes multifactor authentication, biometric identifiers, and other security tools. Like all of those other tools, it remains vulnerable to errors by users and developers—risks that of course also apply to efforts to build systems that provide third-party access.

---

[27] See, for example, A. Lenstra, J.P. Hughes, M. Augier, J.W. Bos, T. Kleinjung, and C. Wachter, 2012, "Ron was wrong, Whit is right," *IACR Technical Report*, https://eprint.iacr.org/2012/064.pdf, and N. Heninger, Z. Durumeric, E. Wustrow, and J.A. Halderman, 2012, "Mining your Ps and Qs: Detection of widespread weak keys in network devices," pp. 204-220 in *Proceedings of the USENIX Security Symposium*, https://www.usenix.org/system/files/tech-schedule/sec12_proceedings.pdf.

3

The Role of Encryption in Protecting Privacy and Civil Liberties

The availability of encryption has come to be recognized as intrinsically bound with rights to privacy, free speech, freedom of association, and freedom of religion, collectively referred to as civil liberties or human rights. Law enforcement agencies are charged with respecting civil liberties, even while working to provide safety and security, which allows individuals to exercise constitutionally protected freedoms.

Government officials concerned about the effects of encryption frequently warn that encryption will disable the government from acting in circumstances where it would be in the public interest to do so. At the same time, opponents of government restrictions on encryption warn about the harmful effects of such restrictions on commerce and on fundamental rights of privacy, speech, and free association, including in repressive regimes. The committee does not seek to resolve these competing claims. It does note, however, that legal and constitutional constraints frequently prevent the United States and many other governments from acting, even when there are competing public interests, and also that rights likewise are not usually absolute.

In the United States, as the Supreme Court has explained, privacy, free speech, freedom of association, and freedom of religion are essential to a functioning democracy, and there is often a convergence of First Amendment rights, Fourth Amendment protections against unreasonable search and seizure, and the protected zones of privacy that stem from these rights. In a case involving undisclosed wiretap surveillance, the Court stated:

> Historically, the struggle for freedom of speech and press in England was bound up with the issue of the scope of the search and seizure power. ... History abundantly documents the tendency of Government—however benevolent and benign its motive—to view with suspicion those who most fervently dispute its policies. Fourth Amendment protections become the more necessary when the targets of official surveillance may be those suspected of unorthodoxy in their political beliefs.[1]

The Court further described how the right to privacy is essential to protecting free speech rights:

> The price of lawful public dissent must not be a dread of subjection to an unchecked surveillance power. Nor must the fear of unauthorized official eavesdropping deter vigorous citizen dissent and discussion of Government action in private conversation. For private dissent, no less than open public discourse, is essential to our free society.[2]

Concern about the effects of government surveillance is a recurring theme in U.S. history. The Church Committee's 1976 report, which detailed abuses of intelligence information involving every president from Franklin Roosevelt through Richard Nixon, warns of the potential chilling effect of government surveillance:

> When Government infringes those rights instead of nurturing and protecting them, the injury spreads far beyond the particular citizens targeted to untold numbers of other Americans who may be intimidated.[3]

Vice President Hubert Humphrey observed in 1967:

> We act differently if we believe we are being observed. If we can never be sure whether or not we are being watched and listened to, all our actions will be altered and our very character will change.[4]

These dangers to free expression posed by government surveillance were also addressed in Justice Sonia Sotoymayor's concurring opinion in United States v. Jones: "Awareness that the Government may be watching chills associational and expressive freedoms. And the Government's

---

[1] *United States v. United States District Court*, 407 U.S. 297, 313-4 (1972).

[2] Ibid., at 314.

[3] Senate Select Committee to Study Government Operations with Respect to Intelligence Activities, 1976, Intelligence Activities and the Rights of Americans, Book II Report No. 94-755, U.S. Senate, April 26, https://www.intelligence.senate.gov/sites/default/files/94755_II.pdf, p. 290.

[4] E.V. Long, 1967, *The Intruders*, with a foreword by Hubert H. Humphrey, p. viii.

unrestrained power to assemble data that reveal private aspects of identity is susceptible to abuse."[5]

Since the explosion of Internet availability and electronic communications capability around the world, exercising of the freedoms of speech and belief, including the right to obtain information, depends more and more on the ability to access the Internet and communicate electronically.[6] As electronic communications and Internet access are subject to electronic surveillance, the right to privacy for one's political, religious, and other communications, opinions, and activities has become even more important.

In particular, as surveillance capabilities have increased, threats to the exercise of these fundamental rights have also increased. Repressive regimes have imposed outright censorship on the Internet and tried to prevent the use of electronic messaging by political opponents and powerful countries have attacked political actors in other countries.

These developments have led to the view that encryption, which protects the privacy of communications and sensitive information, has become an intrinsic part of the rights to freedoms of speech and belief.[7] Some would also contend that regulation of encryption amounts to a restriction on the manner by which citizens represent their own expression. In practice, encryption has come to play a more and more critical role in the work of journalists, human rights advocates, lawyers, public activists, and private communities of faith and opinion.[8]

Even in democracies that recognize the rule of law, the ability to

---

[5] 132 S. Ct. 945, 956 (2012).

[6] As explained by the United Nations Special Rapporteur on the promotion and protection of the right to freedom of opinion and expression,

> The Internet has profound value for freedom of opinion and expression, as it magnifies the voice and multiplies the information within reach of everyone who has access to it. Within a brief period, it has become the central global public forum. As such, an open and secure Internet should be counted among the leading prerequisites for the enjoyment of the freedom of expression today. See David Kaye, 2015, *Report of the Special Rapporteur on the Promotion and Protection of the Right to Freedom of Opinion and Expression: A/HRC/29/32*, Report to the Human Rights Council, May 22, p. 5.

[7] "Encryption and anonymity provide individuals and groups with a zone of privacy online to hold opinions and exercise freedom of expression without arbitrary and unlawful interference or attacks." D. Kaye, 2015, *Report of the Special Rapporteur on the Promotion and Protection of the Right to Freedom of Opinion and Expression: A/HRC/29/32*, Report to the Human Rights Council, May 22, p. 7.

[8] In the United States, most of the major media have adopted methods using encryption to enable secure communication between sources and journalists. (See for example, https://www.nytimes.com/newsgraphics/2016/news-tips/.) The State Department has recognized the use of encrypted communications by human rights advocates and political dissenters in repressive countries as so important that the U.S. government has provided important support for the use of encryption technology. See D. Kaye, 2015, *Report of the Special Rapporteur on the Promotion and Protection of the Right to Freedom of Opinion and Expression: A/HRC/29/32*, Report to the Human Rights Council, May 22.

engage in secure communications is an important protection for civil liberties. Moreover, those in such countries also face threats from actions sponsored by other nations as well as potentially from domestic political opponents. In addition, citizens of these democracies who travel in other countries are affected by the state of civil liberties and the rule of law there.

This report considers whether technical measures required by law to provide the government with access to specific plaintext pursuant to a valid and proper warrant could weaken the security of other encrypted information belonging to other individuals. If so, such measures may negatively impact the civil liberties or human rights of those individuals who are not targeted by the particular warrant. At a minimum, the availability of encryption for communications protects against the chill to free speech stemming from the fear of illegal government surveillance.[9]

There are also situations where law enforcement claims the legal right to obtain information without a warrant. In some of those situations, the Supreme Court has agreed with law enforcement, in others the Supreme Court has disagreed with law enforcement, and in still others, there remains some vagueness or uncertainty. Individuals may encrypt their information to safeguard against circumstances where the government does not have a warrant and the law regarding government access is unclear.

At the same time, as discussed in Chapter 4, criminals and terrorists use encryption to hide their activities from law enforcement and take actions that negatively impact the security of law-abiding individuals.

Solutions, therefore, must take into account both the needs for individuals to be able to have their privacy and civil liberties protected from intrusive government encroachment and individuals' interests in protecting against both criminal actors and threats to national security.

---

[9] Public perception of the risk of illegal government surveillance has been shaped by recent developments. For example, major thefts of documents from U.S. government agencies concerning their surveillance capabilities have generated widespread, although not always completely accurate, news coverage.

4

Information Needs of Law Enforcement and the Intelligence Community

As human activity has become increasingly digital, so too have crime and criminal evidence. Criminals increasingly take advantage of widespread encryption—often available by default—to facilitate drug trafficking, online child exploitation, human trafficking, and other crimes, and to impede detection, apprehension, or prosecution. In addition, the country faces myriad national security threats from terrorist groups and foreign rivals.

This chapter explores the interplay between the needs of law enforcement to obtain plaintext and potential alternatives to plaintext if it cannot be obtained because it is encrypted. Chapter 5 looks at options for law enforcement to obtain access to plaintext that is now encrypted.

GOALS OF LAW ENFORCEMENT OFFICIALS AND INTELLIGENCE ANALYSTS

Law enforcement officials and intelligence analysts have different missions and work with different tools, legal frameworks, and norms, but both are attempting to piece together events or future plans from incomplete or fragmented information.

The role of a criminal investigator is to identify the guilty party and obtain evidence for a conviction. In some cases, this involves exoneration of previous suspects once exculpatory evidence is uncovered. An investigator generally aims to gather evidence needed to bring a successful prosecution against a person or organization responsible for a crime or to disrupt or prevent criminal activity. In order to successfully prosecute, either by trial or through a plea deal, the investigator must supply evidence of guilty actions and intentions beyond a reasonable doubt.[1] Rules derived from constitutional and statutory law as interpreted by courts govern the ways in which investigators can access evidence, how they must share the evidence they gather with the defense, and how they must prove the reliability of the evidence in order to permit it to be introduced in court.

An intelligence analyst, by contrast, has goals that are less about proving a case in court and more about gathering information for a variety of purposes, whether about a particular adversary or to describe developments to policy makers. Foreign intelligence material is gathered, analyzed, and disseminated according to a set of policies and oversight controls within each intelligence agency. The gathering itself makes use of a broad range of techniques and tools, including some not available to law enforcement agencies.[2] The degree of confidence that accompanies a particular assessment will vary, and it is up to the decision maker to assess its quality. Intelligence information and the sources and methods used to gather it are kept secret, and the targets of intelligence gathering are, unlike in criminal investigations, not usually afforded notice.

THE VOLUME AND DIVERSITY OF INFORMATION RELEVANT TO LAW ENFORCEMENT AND THE INTELLIGENCE COMMUNITY

The ways people communicate, engage in commerce, and otherwise live their lives create information across a wide range of networks, devices, and communications streams. For example, the Pew Foundation has reported that only 8 percent of U.S. adults were on social media in 2005, 47 percent in 2010, and 69 percent in 2016.[3] As is discussed below, this has two significant consequences for investigations: (1) the role of digital information in investigations is growing, and therefore loss of access owing to encryption has a greater impact, and (2) a wider variety and volume of digital information that may not be encrypted is also becoming available.

---

[1] Most cases in the criminal justice system are settled through plea negotiations. Nevertheless, the evidence must be sufficient to convince a defendant to accept a plea.

[2] For example, U.S. intelligence agencies working outside the United States could subvert the supply chain for technology used by a foreign intelligence target or leverage skills and computing power for decryption purposes without making these available to the law enforcement community more broadly.

[3] Pew Research Center, 2017, "Social Media Fact Sheet," January 12, http://www.pewinternet.org/fact-sheet/social-media/.

The new, varied, and growing pool of relevant information that may be available to investigators has provided the government with new resources and new challenges. In some cases, law enforcement officials are able to track individual locations through tools such as cell towers, transit passes, license plate readers, and geo-coded photographs and social media postings. Metadata, information about communications, or digital files other than their content can provide valuable information in some circumstances. Many apps capture metadata that often includes the user's location; this source of information was not available to investigators a decade ago. The widespread use of cloud storage means that law enforcement has another potential source of evidence to turn to when they do not have access to the data on devices, either because the device is unavailable or the data on the device is encrypted. Not all of this digital information will be useful, however. Because storage is cheap or even free, people keep all sorts of non-noteworthy electronic documents forever.

At the same time, some forms of evidence that were previously generated and maintained in hard copy now exist only digitally. In some instances, this means that evidence found in new technologies is not necessarily in addition to, but rather may be instead of, former sources of evidence.

Some of that information is relevant to the mission of government agencies responsible for protecting the public. In the law enforcement world, that subset is generally thought of as evidence of a crime. For intelligence agencies seeking foreign intelligence,[4] it is source material for collection. In either case, any reduction in access to that pool of relevant information may reduce their effectiveness at accomplishing their mission.

Investigators and analysts are seeking access to relevant information from a range of sources. Relevant information comes in many different forms. The prevailing conceptual model divides law enforcement needs into two broad categories: evidence in motion and evidence at rest. Evidence at rest can be relevant plaintext stored on a device or relevant plaintext stored on servers operated by a service provider or other third party. Evidence in motion is the target of real-time communications or data intercepts. This can take a traditional form, such as a phone call, or a cutting-edge form, such as messages exchanged over encrypted messaging applications like Signal.

Information used in investigations is sometimes divided into content and noncontent, or metadata. Metadata is generally defined as data that provides information about other data. When the term metadata arises

---

[4] Foreign intelligence is "information relating to the capabilities, intentions, or activities of foreign governments or elements thereof, foreign organizations, or foreign persons, or international terrorist activities" (50 U.S. Code § 303).

in the encryption debate, it has multiple related meanings that are not always carefully distinguished.

One use of the term metadata comes from electronic surveillance law, in which a distinction is drawn between the protections afforded to communications content and those afforded to the noncontent, or metadata, associated with the content. For example, information about the phone numbers of parties to a call is distinguished from recordings of the call obtained from a wiretap.[5] This distinction stems from law and court cases of the telephony era, and relies in part on the third-party doctrine, which holds that people do not have a reasonable expectation of privacy in information they voluntarily provide to third parties—in this case the telephone numbers given to the carrier so that the call can be placed.

In the context of government access to encrypted information and possible alternatives, the term metadata also refers more broadly to information that is associated with content that may be accessible in an unencrypted form even if the content itself is encrypted. Not all metadata is necessarily covered by the third-party doctrine; for example, a time stamp recorded when an encrypted file is created on a computer would be considered metadata about that file but would not have been provided to a third party if the computer is owned by the target of the investigation. Finally, metadata is sometimes used to refer to any noncontent information, even if not necessarily associated with a specific piece of encrypted data, that may be useful as an alternative source of information for an investigation if the encrypted data cannot be decrypted.

In addition to the communications metadata discussed above, a number of other forms of metadata are created by computer systems, including the following:

- Event-related data associated with communications streams provides information about the time, date, payload amount, and other details about a particular communications event but not the content.
- Addressing data can often be used to identify who is communicating, where they are located, and—depending on the specificity of the address—what content they are consuming (e.g., a particular URL).
- Metadata associated with a particular digital file, like the creation date, creation device, and other information stored with the content of the file, but separate from it, can provide information about when and where activity occurred.

---

[5] The boundary between content and noncontent is less clear for Internet protocol (IP)-based communications. See S.M. Bellovin et al., 2016, "It's too complicated: How the Internet upends Katz, Smith, and electronic surveillance law," *Harvard Journal of Law and Technology* 30(1).

• Service logs and telemetry data created in the normal course of supporting software and reporting bugs can provide information on a user's digital activity using that software.[6]

Metadata may not be meaningfully available in all cases. Some metadata is ephemeral and thus not available to investigators after the fact. In other cases, metadata may exist but its existence may not be known to investigators. Also, some kinds of metadata can be altered if one has the right tools and know-how, which may reduce its evidentiary value.

Some metadata may also be encrypted by either the service provider that creates it or only available to investigators as part of a communications stream or on a storage device that is itself encrypted. Other metadata, such as routing data—Internet Protocol (IP) address, e-mail address, or phone number—cannot easily be encrypted.

ENCRYPTION AS AN IMPEDIMENT TO INVESTIGATIONS

Encryption has significantly reduced the amount of plaintext that investigators can access. Several factors are responsible for this. One is a desire to provide robust encryption to individuals and organizations. Another is the effort being made by some companies to reduce their ability to access customer information or encryption keys. Such moves might be made for a variety of reasons. For example, a company might wish to eliminate the possibility that an error will cause customer data to leak (and thereby to reduce liability for such a loss) or seek to gain the trust of a customer who fears the provider might snoop on the customer's trade secrets for a business advantage.

A recent Center for Strategic and International Studies report[7] observed that the share of unrecoverable encryption as a share of total message traffic is likely to grow as instant messaging becomes increasingly dominant. The report notes that 3 of the top 12 mobile messaging apps have enabled end-to-end encryption by default. It estimates that 18 percent of message traffic is encrypted today and that this will grow to 22 percent by 2019 based on projected growth in the use of instant messaging. The report also estimates that roughly 47 percent of all smartphones and tablets in the United States have full disk encryption and observes that if Android devices adopt universal disk encryption, the vast majority

---

[6] National Academies of Sciences, Engineering, and Medicine, 2016, *Exploring Encryption and Potential Mechanisms for Authorized Government Access to Plaintext: Proceedings of a Workshop*, The National Academies Press, Washington D.C., p. 44.

[7] J.A. Lewis, D.E. Zheng, and W.A. Carter, 2017, *Effect of Encryption of Lawful Access to Communications and Data: A Report of the CSIS Technology Policy Program*, https://www.csis.org/analysis/effect-encryption-lawful-access-communications-and-data.

of smartphones in the world would appear to present serious barriers to law enforcement and intelligence agencies access.

Some, but certainly not all, of the data will remain accessible because data is often stored in more than one place. For example, although someone's Gmail messages may be inaccessible from a locked and encrypted phone, these same messages will be stored on Google's servers. Customer data stored by U.S. providers is, however, sometimes stored outside the United States. Whether U.S. providers can be compelled by warrant under current law to provide data stored overseas is currently before the U.S. Supreme Court.[8]

Law enforcement agencies have been reporting they are increasingly unable to unlock encrypted phones. In November 11, 2016, testimony to this committee, then–Federal Bureau of Investigation (FBI) General Counsel James Baker reported that for fiscal year 2016, the FBI had encountered passcodes on 2,095 of the 6,814 mobile devices examined by its forensic laboratories. They were able to break into 1,210 of the locked phones, leaving 885 that could not be accessed. The information Baker presented neither addressed the nature of the crimes involved nor whether the crimes were solved using other techniques. More recent figures were provided by Deputy Attorney General Rod Rosenstein in October 10, 2017, remarks at a U.S. Naval Academy conference: "Over the past year, the FBI was unable to access about 7,500 mobile devices submitted to its Computer Analysis and Response Team, even though there was legal authority to do so."[9] Similar figures were reported by FBI director Christopher Wray in an October 22, 2017, speech to the International Association of Chiefs of Police conference in Philadelphia, Pennsylvania. He pointed to more than 6,900 devices from which federal agents were unable to access the contents. Wray described it as a "huge problem . . . that impacts investigations across the board—narcotics, human trafficking, counterterrorism, counterintelligence, gangs, organized crime, child exploitation."[10]

In November 2016, the Manhattan District Attorney's Office reported that "423 Apple iPhones and iPads lawfully seized since October 2014 remain inaccessible due to default device encryption" and that 10 percent

---

[8] *United States v. Microsoft Corp.*, S.C. Docket No. 17-2.

[9] R.J. Rosenstein, 2017, "Deputy Attorney General Rod J. Rosenstein Delivers Remarks on Encryption at the United States Naval Academy: Remarks as prepared for delivery," October 10, https://www.justice.gov/opa/speech/deputy-attorney-general-rod-j-rosenstein-delivers-remarks-encryption-united-states-naval.

[10] M. Balsamo, 2017, "FBI couldn't access nearly 7K devices because of encryption," *Washington Post*, October 22.

of these devices "pertain to homicide or attempted murder cases."[11] That report also cites data from several other states, counties, and cities on the number or rate of locked devices and locked devices that could not be opened. In November 2017, the office reported that the number of locked and encrypted smartphones received by its digital forensics unit has increased steadily since 2014, reaching over half of all devices received. In the first 10 months of 2017, 1,283 smartphones were received by the office's forensics unit; 466 of the 665 phones running iOS were locked, and 236 of the 618 phones running Android were locked. Also, according to the 2017 report, 160 state and local law enforcement agencies from 37 states that have started to track locked devices report a total number in the thousands.[12]

The U.S. Department of Justice's National Strategy on Child Exploitation Prevention and Interdiction Working Group has looked at the impact of encryption in child pornography investigations. It conducted a survey in late 2015 to early 2016 of "more than 1,000 federal, state, local, and tribal investigators; law enforcement managers; prosecutors; analysts; forensic examiners; victim service providers; and [Department of Justice] grant recipients." In the survey, more than 30 percent of respondents reported that the use of encryption by child pornography offenders has significantly increased.[13]

The data cited above strongly suggest that widespread encryption is having a serious and growing negative impact on the ability of law enforcement to collect relevant plaintext.

Although Director Wray provided a broad characterization of the crimes whose investigation is being impeded, and one can make assumptions about the nature of the cases being pursued by the Child Exploitation Prevention and Interdiction Working Group, there remains a lack of specific data about what kinds of investigations are being impeded and the extent to which investigations were successful by pursuing other routes.

The Administrative Office of the U.S. Courts reports annually on the number of federal and state wiretaps and the number of times that encryption is encountered. The 2016 report indicates that of the 3,168 state and federal wiretaps authorized that year, encryption was encountered in 57 state wiretaps and 68 federal wiretaps. Officials were unable to deci-

---

[11] Manhattan District Attorney's Office, 2016, *Report of the Manhattan District Attorney's Office on Smartphone Encryption and Public Safety: An Update to the November 2015 Report*, November, http://manhattanda.org/smartphone-encryption.

[12] Manhattan District Attorney's Office, 2017, *Third Report of the Manhattan District Attorney's Office on Smartphone Encryption and Public Safety*, New York, N.Y., November.

[13] U.S. Department of Justice, 2016, *The National Strategy for Child Exploitation Prevention and Interdiction: Report to Congress*, https://www.justice.gov/psc/file/842411/download.

pher messages in 48 of the state and 53 of the federal wiretaps.[14] It cannot be discerned from this information how often a wiretap was not sought because the data being sought was known to be encrypted nor what impact the inability to decrypt messages had on investigations. Finally, it is worth noting that a comparison of the number of wiretaps reported in the U.S. courts reports and those reported by service providers in their transparency reports suggests that the number of wiretaps (and thus, potentially, the number of instances where encryption was encountered) may be underreported by more than a factor of 2.[15]

Unfortunately, there are not more comprehensive and systemic data on the incidence and impact of encryption. Although existing data clearly show that encryption is being encountered with increasing frequency, the figures above do not give a clear picture of how frequently an inability to access information seriously hinders investigations and prosecutions. It is not straightforward to collect such data: it is time consuming, assessments of impact are inherently subjective, data sources are highly distributed, and there is no formal infrastructure in place for collection or reporting, especially at the state and local levels.

Statistics tell only one part of the story. The Manhattan District Attorney's Office report describes how it is working with federal, state, and local partners to collect case-related information. The report cites examples collected by National Domestic Communications Assistance Center (NDCAC) of cases that could not be solved, including a violent home invasion in Louisiana; homicides in Massachusetts, Missouri, and New Jersey; identity theft and fraud in Missouri; a violent street gang investigation in Minnesota; and a child sexual assault in Tennessee.

To illustrate the national security challenges posed by encryption, 2015 testimony to the Senate Judiciary Committee by then–FBI Director James Comey and then–Deputy Attorney General Sally Quillian Yates described how encryption is used when recruiting terrorists:

> With the widespread horizontal distribution of social media, terrorists can spot, assess, recruit, and radicalize vulnerable individuals of all ages in the United States either to travel or to conduct a homeland attack. As a result, foreign terrorist organizations now have direct access into the United States like never before. For example, in recent arrests, a group of individuals was contacted by a known ISIL supporter who had already successfully traveled to Syria and encouraged them to do the same. Some of these conversations occur in publicly accessed social networking sites,

---

[14] Administrative Office of the U.S. Courts, 2016, *Wiretap Report 2016*, December 31, http://www.uscourts.gov/statistics-reports/wiretap-report-2016.

[15] A. Gidari, 2017, "Just Security," July 6, https://www.justsecurity.org/24427/wiretap-numbers-add.

but others take place via private messaging platforms. These encrypted direct messaging platforms are tremendously problematic when used by terrorist plotters.[16]

The timeliness of plaintext recovery matters. The extent to which it matters will differ depending on the nature of the investigation. For example, information is, generally speaking, needed more urgently in an investigation intended to prevent a crime than one collecting evidence after the fact. Similarly, it may be critical in some cases to collect evidence quickly to identify and apprehend a suspect, while in others, the goal may be to gather evidence to support a prosecution after a suspect has been identified.

Further, information is not fungible. It is not always possible to accomplish a particular aim with different information, either content or metadata, from another source. Location information and other metadata are extremely useful for understanding patterns and networks of people, but less so for motivations and plans. Location information or metadata would be very useful if the government's object were to determine where a particular exchange of packages occurred, for example, but would be less useful in determining what was in the packages. The law enforcement community thus argues that it is more difficult to convince a jury of criminal intent using metadata evidence than with content evidence.

It is unclear how manageable the loss of access to information owing to encryption is for the intelligence community, but it is likely to be less of a game-changer for a variety of reasons. At least with regard to nation-state targets, the intelligence community has long been confronted by the use of encryption. The intelligence community has substantially more resources and can develop highly specialized solutions that do not need to be scalable. The intelligence community also typically operates outside the United States and thus under more permissive rules than those that govern domestic law enforcement activities. Finally, intelligence analysis is often based on inferred conclusions and is not held to a standard of beyond a reasonable doubt.

Encryption is not the only impediment to law enforcement use of relevant plaintext; there are significant training, resource, capacity, and technology barriers to digital evidence-gathering. The challenge will grow as new technologies, and thus sources of information, are introduced. In addition, law enforcement must deal with a wide array of firms that may hold data relevant to an investigation and the diverse range of procedures

---

[16] J. Comey, 2015, "Going Dark: Encryption, Technology, and the Balances Between Public Safety and Privacy: Joint Statement with Deputy Attorney General Sally Quillian Yates Before the Senate Judiciary Committee," Federal Bureau of Investigation, July 8, https://www.fbi.gov/news/testimony/going-dark-encryption-technology-and-the-balances-between-public-safety-and-privacy.

these firms will put in place for working with law enforcement. A related challenge is that the novelty of the technology and associated legal issues means that both law enforcement agencies and companies are likely to encounter unsettled law—the resolution of which can delay the government's access to data. Finally, companies are increasingly distributing data across multinational networks—for example, to store data closer to where it is used. As a result, some relevant plaintext in domestic cases is accessible only through international legal mechanisms that may be slow and cumbersome, as well as unfamiliar to most state and local law enforcement investigators. See the introduction to Chapter 6.

THE PRACTICAL UTILITY OF ALTERNATIVES TO EXCEPTIONAL ACCESS

As investigators and analysts lose access to some relevant plaintext because of encryption, they will look to alternative ways to accomplish their goals. Put another way, the real issue for investigators is not whether they can obtain needed information from a particular source but whether they can obtain the needed information from some source in a sufficiently reliable, timely, and scalable manner. In some cases, this will be traditional sources like witness interviews, physical surveillance, or biological evidence. In other cases, investigators turn to other sectors of the digital world. Even as encryption hampers access to some evidence, new sources of evidence are becoming available. At the same time, some forms of evidence that were previously generated and maintained in hard copy now exist only digitally. One key issue is how useful the new forms of evidence are. Another is how the costs and benefits of exploiting those new sources compare to those from compelled decryption through an exceptional access mechanism. Finally, in some cases, technology enables law enforcement to gather and utilize evidence far more cheaply and efficiently than has been possible in the past.[17]

---

[17] See, for example, Justice Samuel Alito's concurring opinion in *United States v. Jones*, 132 S.Ct. 945 (2012):

> Traditional surveillance for any extended period of time was difficult and costly and therefore rarely undertaken. The surveillance at issue in this case—constant monitoring of the location of a vehicle for four weeks—would have required a large team of agents, multiple vehicles, and perhaps aerial assistance.

An estimate of such costs by Bankston and Soltani, which looked at the cost of acquiring location information (but not analyzing it), shows that the cost of tracking a suspect has dropped dramatically as a result of communications technology. They estimate that tracking using a team of plainclothes police and unmarked cars would be about $275 an hour. A GPS device placed on a suspect's car would cost only $10 an hour (but note that a search warrant is required to do this), while tracking a suspect using their cell phone signal would

Broadly, the new sources of digital information potentially useful for law enforcement fall into three categories: (1) gaining access to content using new techniques, (2) exploiting new sources for content that might supplement or substitute for plaintext, and (3) using metadata.

If access to content is hampered by encryption, investigators can attempt to gain access without the cooperation of the manufacturer or service provider by intruding into a system where plaintext is resident, but proper legal authority and oversight is necessary. Such "lawful hacking" has a range of benefits and challenges on its own—in particular, it tends not to be scalable and is best applied to a small number of targeted devices. See the section "Legal Aspects of Lawful Hacking" in Chapter 5 for more discussion.

Current and emerging technologies offer potential new sources for content and metadata. Some alternative sources of plaintext as well as kinds and sources of metadata are enumerated below with the objective of giving the reader an understanding of the alternatives and their utility. Application of the framework proposed by the committee will involve deeper examination of specific solutions. Some possible alternative sources include the following:

- Many devices and operating systems provide for online or cloud storage of some customer information. Provided there are business reasons to keep content unencrypted or business requirements or customer demand to recover data when passwords are forgotten, much of this data should be available with appropriate legal demands. Of course, the cloud data is not always complete or current, and its presence or absence will depend on what backup features have been implemented and what options the device owner has selected. Moreover, it is technically possible for providers to implement encryption so that they do not have access to decryption keys, and some services provide this option.
- Stored e-mail, photos, and social network posts can all provide information on interests, intentions, activities, and intentions. Their availability to investigators will depend on the data-retention policies of the service providers.
- The location history of mobile phone users can be obtained from cell service providers. In addition, many smartphone applications themselves capture location information and transmit it to the providers of services associated with those applications.
- Smartphones often synchronize contacts and other data with auto-

---

be even cheaper. See K.S. Bankston and A. Soltani, 2013, "Tiny constables and the cost of surveillance: Making cents out of United States v. Jones," *Yale Law Journal Forum* 123:335.

mobile infotainment systems and telematics systems. These systems also store information about vehicle usage.

- "Connected homes" contain data on smart thermostats and appliances. Many devices in the home, such as smart televisions and personal assistants, continuously listen for and respond to voice commands and may retain buffered information about the user's activity. Service providers are adopting technical measures to limit data retention to protect user privacy and have asserted constitutional defenses to producing such data, however, and its future utility is not certain.
- Worn or implanted technology, such as fitness monitors and pacemakers and insulin pumps controlled from smartphones, provide information about the activities of their users and may produce useful evidence in some cases.[18]

Of course companies could choose to limit the collection of such information if, for example, customers express concerns about privacy or the ability of the government to obtain this information and assuming it is not necessary for their service or business model.

As discussed above, metadata is another alternative to content that at present is not usually encrypted. It is especially valuable for providing information about "who," "where," and "when." For example, "to" and "from" Internet protocol addresses can be used to map criminal networks. Without access to the content of messages and stored data, one cannot directly determine "what"—such as the plans and intentions of criminals—although this information can sometimes be inferred from metadata.

In each instance where an alternative source of evidence is identified, then, it is reasonable to ask (1) the extent to which it can meet law enforcement needs and (2) how much additional effort, training, or cost it will take to gather the alternative evidence as compared to exceptional access to plaintext.

One issue that arises in comparing alternatives is the appropriate baseline. One view is to ask to what extent alternative sources can replace plaintext now inaccessible owing to encryption. Another is to take into account the recent growth of opportunities for government surveillance—such as widespread adoption of cellphones in the 1990s and smartphones a decade later—that may help offset information lost to encryption. A third perspective is to consider the growing importance of digital evidence in all investigations. Beyond these points, many, if not all, of the questions

---

[18] G. Ballenger, 2017, "New form of law enforcement investigation hits close to the heart," *Slate*, July 19, http://www.slate.com/blogs/future_tense/2017/07/19/a_man_s_pacemaker_data_will_be_used_against_him_in_court.html.

in the framework set forth in Chapter 7 are relevant to evaluating the net costs and benefits of proposed alternatives to accessing encrypted content.

Whatever the baseline, it will be important to rigorously evaluate the impacts of encryption, proposed approaches for exceptional access, and the utility and cost of proposed alternatives. Such an effort would be facilitated by more rigorous data collection about the impact of encryption on federal, state, and local law enforcement and the effectiveness and costs of alternatives.

5

Options for Accessing Plaintext

OPTIONS FOR ACCESSING PLAINTEXT

As discussed in Chapter 1, the options for ensuring access to plaintext fall into the following broad categories:

- Take no legislative action but potentially pursue technical, law enforcement, and legal options to obtain or compel cooperation of target;
- Provide additional resources to access plaintext;
- Enact legislation that requires that device vendors or service providers provide government access to plaintext without specifying the technical means of doing so; and
- Enact legislation requiring a particular technical approach.

As noted previously, these are not necessarily mutually exclusive; for example, the second option can be pursued regardless of or in addition to the other three options.

Each of these categories may involve some combination of (1) legal and policy changes, (2) technical means, and (3) provision of additional financial or technical support. The sections that follow explain each of these three areas. Some are available today (but could be enhanced with additional resources), while others require new technologies, major investments, or legal changes. Although some of these options have been studied—some over a period of almost two decades—all but the status quo represent new initiatives that would undoubtedly lead to new technical, market, and legal responses if implemented. The final section of this chapter considers some of the issues that would arise with legislation mandating government access.

LEGAL TOOLS FOR OBTAINING PLAINTEXT WITHIN THE CURRENT LEGISLATIVE FRAMEWORK

Even without new legislation mandating government access, there are several legal avenues currently available to the government that may enable it to decrypt the information. This section discusses legal issues that arise in those situations.

Compelled Disclosure of Biometric Identifiers or Passcodes

There are many different situations in which the government has legal authority to obtain information, but where access to the information or the meaning of the information may be defeated by encryption technologies. For example, in many cases, the government may legally obtain a computer or handheld device that requires a fingerprint or other biometric information or passcode for access. Even where access to the computer or device is not limited, a particular file on a computer or device may be protected by a passcode or other means. The government may also have the legal authority to seize and obtain information stored in other places, like the cloud, but accessing such information may nevertheless require a biometric identifier or passcode.

The legal avenues available to the government in these cases depend in part on whether the information is protected by a biometric identifier or by a passcode as well as whether the government is seeking information directly from the user or from a third party like the provider.

Biometric Identifiers

Where the information is protected by a biometric identifier and the user of a device is in custody or otherwise available, the government may seek to compel the user to provide a fingerprint or other biometric data to unlock a device and allow access to the data within.

At the moment, the law is reasonably well settled that the government may obtain such an order in the context of certain physical acts.[1] As the Supreme Court held in United States v. Hubbell, 530 U.S. 27, 34-35 (2000), "even though the act may provide incriminating evidence, a criminal

---

[1] *Holt v. United States*, 218 U.S. 245 (1910); *Schmerber v. California*, 384 U.S. 757, 764 (1966); *United States v. Dionisio*, 410 U.S. 1, 5-6 (1973); *Doe v. United States*, 487 U.S. 201 (1988).

suspect may be compelled to put on a shirt, to provide a blood sample or handwriting exemplar, or to make a recording of his voice."

To be sure, complexities may arise under the Fifth Amendment when the act of providing the fingerprint could be deemed to be testimonial—for example, an implicit admission that the phone in question belongs to the subject—but obtaining a fingerprint per se, or compelling someone to touch a fingerprint sensor, is likely not itself a testimonial act protected by the Fifth Amendment, although there may be exceptions.[2]

As one court of appeals has explained,

> [A]n act of production can be testimonial when that act conveys some explicit or implicit statement of fact that certain materials exist, are in the subpoenaed individual's possession or control, or are authentic. The touchstone of whether an act of production is testimonial is whether the government compels the individual to use "the contents of his own mind" to explicitly or implicitly communicate some statement of fact. Put another way, the Court has marked out two ways in which an act of production is not testimonial. First, the Fifth Amendment privilege is not triggered where the Government merely compels some physical act, i.e. where the individual is not called upon to make use of the contents of his or her mind. The most famous example is the key to the lock of a strongbox containing documents, but the Court has also used this rationale in a variety of other contexts. Second, under the "foregone conclusion" doctrine, an act of production is not testimonial—even if the act conveys a fact regarding the existence or location, possession, or authenticity of the subpoenaed materials—if the Government can show with "reasonable particularity" that, at the time it sought to compel the act of production, it already knew of the materials, thereby making any testimonial aspect a "foregone conclusion."[3]

There could be practical limits as well, of course, because some hardware devices are designed to remain locked after several failed attempts to open them biometrically—for example, by then requiring that the passcode be entered. And of course, not all users enable biometric features, and the features can be readily disabled.

---

[2] For a discussion of some of the complexities, see K. Goldman, 2015, "Biometric passwords and the privileged against self-incrimination," *Cardozo Arts & Entertainment Law Journal* 33:211; O. Kerr, 2016, "Can warrants for digital evidence also require fingerprints to unlock phones?," *Washington Post*, October 19; and O. Kerr, 2016, "The Fifth Amendment and Touch ID," *Washington Post*, October 21.

[3] In *re Grand Jury Subpoena Duces Tecum Dated March 25, 2011*, 670 F.3d 1335, 1345-46 (11th Cir. 2012).

Passcodes

The situation is almost exactly reversed when it comes to compelled production of a passcode. In most situations, the law does not allow the government to compel disclosure of a passcode. Unlike a biometric marker, disclosing a passcode is generally understood as a testimonial act protected by the Fifth Amendment. Thus, under current case law, although providing a fingerprint may resemble providing a physical key to a safe, disclosing a passcode is more like revealing the combination to a safe, which is protected.[4] At the same time, there may be circumstances where someone other than the owner in the case of a privately owned device or a corporation in the case of a business-owned device, knows the passcode and in that situation, the government could compel production of the passcode because that individual or organization would not have a Fifth Amendment right to refuse disclosure.

Compelled Assistance by Third Parties and Related Issues

Where the government cannot obtain the assistance of the user of a device to defeat encryption, it may also seek assistance from third parties, such as the manufacturer of a device or the provider of a software operating system. To date, issues in this area have usually arisen under the All Writs Act (28 U.S.C. §1651); its application, however, is currently unsettled law. Issues may also arise under the "technical assistance" provisions of the Wiretap Act (8 U.S.C. §2511). Another option for the government is "lawful hacking," which typically does not require compelled assistance from a third party, but accomplishes some of the same results and may raise some of the same questions. One controversy that arises in connection with compelled assistance is whether and on what time scale providers should be allowed to disclose that such assistance has been provided.

All Writs Act

Although the use of the All Writs Act in a decryption case came to public prominence in connection with efforts by the Federal Bureau of Investigation (FBI) to compel Apple to decrypt the phone of a dead terrorist in the San Bernardino, California, case, the act has long been used to compel assistance from third parties in implementing surveillance orders obtained by the government. In 1977, the Supreme Court addressed such technical assistance in *U.S. v. New York Tel. Co.*,[5] where it held that the

---

[4] See *Doe v. U.S.*, 487 U.S. 201 (1988) at 210 n.9.
[5] 434 U.S. 159 (1977).

All Writs Act, which allows federal courts to "issue all writs necessary or appropriate in aid of their respective jurisdictions and agreeable to the usages and principles of law,"[6] could be used to compel a telephone company to assist with installation of a pen register, a mechanism to record the telephone numbers called by the phone. The pen register itself was authorized under Federal Rule of Criminal Procedure 41, but that rule did not explicitly require telephone companies to provide technical assistance in installing a pen register. In deciding that the government could invoke the All Writs Act to compel assistance, the Supreme Court noted that the Wiretap Act contains a provision requiring companies to provide technical assistance. The Court explained that in light of the Wiretap Act's "direct command to federal courts to compel, upon request, any assistance necessary to accomplish an electronic interception, it would be remarkable if Congress thought it beyond the power of the federal courts to exercise, where required, a discretionary authority to order telephone companies to assist in the installation and operation of pen registers, which accomplish a far lesser invasion of privacy."

The government has started using the All Writs Act to seek considerably more in the way of technical assistance from providers or others to defeat encryption. To what extent the act applies to such cases and what kind of assistance can be compelled by the act is unsettled by the courts; Congress could conceivably step in to clarify as well. In the Eastern District of New York, for example, the Department of Justice and Apple engaged in a dispute about whether Apple could be compelled to unlock an iPhone for which there was a federal search warrant. The government relied on the All Writs Act and *New York Tel. Co.*, while Apple claimed that the All Writs Act does not apply as a result of Communications Assistance for Law Enforcement Act (CALEA),[7] a 1994 statute that requires telecommunications providers to maintain their networks in certain ways that allow for wiretapping, but does not apply to stored data on a handset. Apple argued that Congress considered and rejected the possibility of imposing mandates for law enforcement access on handset device providers when it adopted CALEA.

Apple's main argument was that the All Writs Act could not be used to compel what Congress declined to address in CALEA—that is, that

---

[6] 28 U.S.C. §1651.

[7] 47 U.S.C. §1001-1010. Under one provision of Commission on Accreditation for Law Enforcement Agencies, Inc. (CALEA), 47 U.S.C. §1002(b)(3), a "telecommunications carrier shall not be responsible for decrypting, or ensuring the government's ability to decrypt, any communication encrypted by a subscriber or customer, unless the encryption was provided by the carrier and the carrier possesses the information necessary to decrypt the communication."

CALEA occupies the field of compelled assistance.[8] In February 2016, a magistrate judge in Brooklyn, New York, ruled for Apple, concluding that "the relief the government seeks" under the All Writs Act "is unavailable," primarily "because Congress has considered legislation that would achieve the same result but has not adopted it" in CALEA.[9] The government's appeal is pending. By contrast, a magistrate judge in the Central District of California reached the opposite conclusion.[10] In this latter case, the FBI used technical means to obtain the data, and the lawsuit was dismissed. There will undoubtedly be more litigation in this area.

Assuming that the government prevails in its interpretation of the All Writs Act and can legally compel companies to provide technical assistance to defeat encryption where the government has a lawful warrant for the encrypted information, the extent and circumstances of such assistance will presumably be worked out on a case-by-case base.

Technical Assistance

As noted above, in applying the All Writs Act in *New York Tel. Co.*, the Supreme Court reasoned by analogy to the "technical assistance" provision in the Wiretap Act. It is therefore possible, in a case involving a wiretap (rather than access to stored data via a search warrant), that the government may seek to compel assistance from providers under that provision. There is today very little publicly available law on the limits of "technical assistance." A divided panel of the Ninth Circuit held that the Wiretap Act could not be used to compel assistance with a wiretap in ways that entirely disabled the communications system for the particular customer targeted by the surveillance. The majority concluded that disabling the system was inconsistent with the statutory command that technical assistance be provided "in such a manner as will protect its secrecy and produce a minimum of interference with the services that such carrier . . . is providing that target of electronic surveillance":

---

[8] See Quinta Jurecic, DOJ and Apple File Briefs in EDNY Encryption Case, Lawfare (Oct. 26, 2015), https://www.lawfareblog.com/doj-and-apple-file-briefs-edny-encryption-case; see also H.R. Rep. 103-827(I), 103d Cong. 2d Sess. at 13 (1994) ("While the Supreme Court has read [18 U.S.C. §2518(4)] as requiring the Federal courts to compel, upon request of the government, 'any assistance necessary to accomplish an electronic interception,' United States v. New York Telephone, 434 U.S. 159, 177 (1977), the question of whether companies have any obligation to design their systems such that they do not impede law enforcement interception has never been adjudicated.").

[9] In re Apple, Inc., 149 F. Supp.3d 341, 344 (E.D.N.Y. 2016).

[10] In the Matter of the Search of an Apple iPhone Seized During the Execution of a Search Warrant on a Black Lexus IS300, California License Plate 35KGD203, 2016 WL 618401 (C.D. Cal. Feb. 16, 2016).

[T]he "a minimum of interference" requirement certainly allows for some level of interference with customers' service in the conducting of surveillance. We need not decide precisely how much interference is permitted. "A minimum of interference" at least precludes total incapacitation of a service while interception is in progress. Put another way, eavesdropping is not performed with "a minimum of interference" if a service is completely shut down as a result of the surveillance.[11]

The majority further concluded that the assistance provision, unlike CALEA, does not require providers to redesign their systems to facilitate government surveillance.

Legal Aspects of Lawful Hacking

An alternative to introducing lawful access mechanisms to defeat encryption is to use what is sometimes referred to as "lawful hacking," which allows investigators to intrude into a computer system and access its content without the need to break encryption. For example, the government may obtain a warrant to secretly insert software on a targeted computer that surreptitiously records every keystroke on a computer. This can be used to capture the suspect's passwords, thus allowing access to everything else.

The idea behind lawful hacking is that "[i]nstead of introducing new vulnerabilities to communications networks and applications, law enforcement should use vulnerabilities already present in the target's communications device to wiretap in the situations where wiretapping is difficult to achieve by other means."[12] It is a technique that has been in use by the FBI since at least the early 2000s. Information must be in plaintext while the device is processing or displaying and is thus susceptible to capture by appropriately tailored malware to defeat or evade the encryption on a subject's device. Although such malware is not guaranteed to work or be sufficient in every circumstance, it is another option that may be effective in many cases.

Some have suggested that despite its limitations and challenges, lawful hacking offers potential middle ground for at least a subset of cases: "This proposal potentially offers an attractive solution to Going Dark challenges, which could theoretically satisfy equities on both sides of the debate."[13]

---

[11] *In re U.S. for an Order Authorizing Roving Interception of Oral Communications*, 349 F.3d 1132 (9th Cir. 2003).

[12] S.M Bellovin et al., 2014, "Lawful hacking: Using existing vulnerabilities for wiretapping on the Internet," *Northwestern Journal of Technology and Intellectual Property* 12:i.

[13] S. Hennessey and N. Weaver, 2016, "A judicial framework for evaluating network investigative techniques," *Lawfare Blog*, July 28, https://www.lawfareblog.com/judicial-framework-evaluating-network-investigative-techniques.

Two important points about this technique should be noted. First, in discussing this technique, the committee is referring only to instances where the government has a lawful warrant to obtain the encrypted information or in the case of foreign intelligence, a Foreign Intelligence Surveillance Act order. Second, by lawful hacking, the committee means the use of techniques that have been authorized by a court pursuant to law.

The legal dimensions of lawful hacking have not been extensively litigated and are still unclear. For example, it is uncertain whether there are circumstances when the government can be compelled to reveal details about the methods in criminal investigations. It is also uncertain how tools used to generate admissible evidence in court would be vetted in some way for its forensic soundness—for example, the government would have to demonstrate that it could reliably extract evidence without altering it.

Are the issues (particularly the legal issues) different for government-supplied and vendor-supplied tools? Would all techniques be widely available, or available only to certain agencies? How would lawful hacking tools be created and distributed? Under what circumstances is the government required to reveal the vulnerabilities it discovered to the companies that developed the products whose vulnerabilities that hacking tools exploit?

Again, the extent and application of such authority is unsettled and will depend on the particular circumstances of the requested order authorizing lawful hacking.

TECHNOLOGICAL APPROACHES FOR ACCESSING PLAINTEXT, LIMITATIONS, AND ALTERNATIVES

This section examines high-level technical options for providing access to plaintext and the associated challenges with each approach. The discussion draws on the basic concepts of cryptography described in Chapter 2. It is not intended to be comprehensive but rather to introduce some major technical options and to illustrate the issues that arise in evaluating the associated benefits and risks.

Approaches to Exceptional Plaintext Access

A number of technical approaches to providing exceptional access to plaintext have been proposed (see, e.g., Box 5.1). The following are the general approaches most commonly discussed and also selected to be representative of the range of potential benefits and shortcomings of technical access schemes.

BOX 5.1
Recent Efforts to Develop Technical Options

Several individuals with backgrounds in security and systems have begun to explore possible technical mechanisms to provide government exceptional access. Three individuals presented their ideas to the committee.

- Ernie Brickell, former chief security architect, Intel Corporation, described ways that protected partitions, a security feature provided by future microprocessor architectures, could be used to provide law enforcement access to devices in their physical possession, provide remote access by law enforcement, or provide key escrowed cryptography for use by applications and non-escrowed cryptography for a set of "allowed" applications.
- Ray Ozzie, former chief technical officer and former chief software architect, Microsoft Corporation, argued that if a user trusts a vendor to update software, the user should be able to trust the vendor to manage keys that can provide exceptional access. He proposed that this extension of the trust model used for software updates could be used to provide government exceptional access to unlock mobile devices. Ozzie also provided the committee with materials describing how this approach could be extended to real-time communications such as messaging.
- Stefan Savage, professor of computer science and engineering, University of California, San Diego, described how phone unlock keys could be stored in hardware and made available via an internal hardware interface together with a "proof-of-effort" lock that together would require physical possession and a time delay before law enforcement could unlock a device.

At a 2016 workshop organized by the National Academies of Sciences, Engineering, and Medicine[1] Butler Lampson, technical fellow at Microsoft, suggested the use of a design that uses a "k out of n model" to improve the security of an exceptional access scheme. In this type of system, the encryption key is itself encrypted with a set of sealing keys for which a set of matched unsealing keys are created and given to trusted escrow agents. The escrowed encryption keys are broken into a number of pieces, n, and a certain number of them, k, must be combined in order to unlock the encryption. Arguing that the risk introduced by such a system would be small relative to broader cybersecurity risks, Lampson acknowledged that its security relies on eliminating technical bugs from the escrow agent computer systems and on trusting the people and institutions that operate each escrow agent.

As discussed in Chapter 2, proposed encryption schemes are not considered ready for deployment until they have undergone careful scrutiny by experts regarding their effectiveness, scalability, and security risks and been subject to real-world testing at realistic scale in the relevant contexts. All three presenters stated that their proposals could help ease security trade-offs while providing government access. None of the proposals presented to the committee provided sufficient detail for a technical evaluation; in any case, the committee was not in a position to perform the necessarily intensive work and did not reach any conclu-

continued

> **BOX 5.1 Continued**
>
> sions about their merits. The framework in Chapter 7 is intended as a guide for such evaluations.
>
> ---
>
> [1] National Academies of Sciences, Engineering, and Medicine, 2016, *Exploring Encryption and Potential Mechanisms for Authorized Government Access to Plaintext: Proceedings of a Workshop*, The National Academies Press, Washington D.C.

Required Vendor Unlock

One proposed approach would require vendors to maintain capabilities to unlock phones or other devices and access the data stored on them. When a law enforcement agency encounters a device that it needs to unlock, it would present an unlock request for a specified device along with the appropriate legal order. The vendor would then be responsible for validating the source of the request and the judicial documents and, depending on how the access arrangement is structured, either the vendor unlocks the phone when it is presented by law enforcement, or it provides the law enforcement agency with a token the agency can use to unlock the phone.

An unlocking scheme could take various forms. The simplest, but riskiest in terms of the potential scale of compromise, would involve a single master key that covers all phones from a vendor or all phones of a particular model. More likely, a scheme would create an unlock token by combining a vendor's signing key with a unique key associated with a unique device identifier that the vendor creates and stores for each phone. The discussion below assumes a scheme of the latter sort.

An unlocking scheme will not provide direct access to prior communications unless they are stored on the phone (and not separately encrypted by the communications application). However, unlocking a phone by authenticating as a user provides much more capability than just access to the data stored on that device. For example, it allows access to remote accounts or services belonging to the device owner (including but not limited to messaging services) and associated data that is not stored on the phone. The scope of what investigators are permitted to access from an unlocked phone would likely be defined by the authorizing court order. In addition, limits could be set by the technical mechanism. At least one proposal for a vendor unlock mechanism includes a provision to freeze the unlocked device and prevent it from being used directly to, for example, access remote accounts or services.

In terms of the process for interacting with law enforcement agencies, large online service operators such as Google, Facebook, and Apple already have processes in place to receive and validate warrants and other law enforcement requests to manage and deliver unencrypted customer data that they hold. By contrast, device vendors such as Apple do not presently have processes in place to provide law enforcement agencies with unlock codes, which would include not only validating law enforcement requests but also managing master signing keys and creating device-specific unlock codes. A workable solution would have to be deployable on billions of devices.

Vendors already have had to address at least some of the technical risks of an unlocking scheme. Most device and operating system vendors already maintain a master key that is used to authenticate software updates. Because the software update capability enables the vendor to modify the device software arbitrarily, vendors already have strong procedures in place to protect these update keys and limit their use.[14] The process and workflow used by vendors in delivering updates is designed to prevent inadequately tested, unapproved, or malicious code in an update and includes controls that keep a single individual from releasing an update. The key used for device unlock would, the argument goes, be handled by a similar system and similar procedures to those used to protect software update keys. If they are to cryptographically authenticate authorized unlock requests, manufacturers will have to store and protect secret signing keys for this purpose. Exposure of these keys would allow anyone to generate unlock tokens on their own. These signing keys, like the keys that manufacturers use to authenticate software updates, therefore, pose a cybersecurity risk and will have to be protected against criminal organizations and foreign agents. So, too, would the system that stores the keys associated with individual devices. A single point of failure could potentially jeopardize the security of millions of devices.

There is an important difference, however, in the ease of use of an update signing key and a key to accomplish exceptional access. Stealing an update signing key does not give an immediate benefit. The only use for the key is to sign a piece of malicious software that will be used to attack a targeted system or systems. And creation of that malicious software requires significant skill if it is to be capable of being deployed to a large number of target systems or a target system whose attributes are unknown, or if it is intended to be long-lived (e.g., to survive past future

---

[14] The software update capability itself cannot be used to unlock a device because, as with well-designed smartphones, a software update can only be installed on an unlocked device.

valid updates to the target system). The impact of such a signed malicious update could be extremely serious, and preventing theft of signing keys is thus a major concern for software vendors.

Stealing an exceptional access key, by contrast, enables a thief, who has physical access to a device, to open it. An attacker might have only temporary access to a device—perhaps at a border crossing, perhaps while the phone is left outside the protected facility during a meeting. If the exceptional access key can be used to decrypt an externally collected image of the device memory, theft of such a key is an especially serious threat. If the exceptional access key can only be used to decrypt the protected physical device (not a memory image) and if the device is rendered inoperable (frozen) by the act of decryption, as was the operating model for one concept presented to the committee, the device owner will at least have an indication that the device has been compromised.

The security risks of the scheme can be partly mitigated if the access scheme is hardware based (see below) in order that an attack against a device unlock mechanism cannot be carried out remotely. This forces a party seeking to unlock a device to have physical possession of that device.

Several operational factors distinguish an unlocking system from a software update system. For one, such a system would most likely be used more often—perhaps several times per day—as compared to the keys used to sign software updates, which are used infrequently by a generally small group of highly trusted individuals. For another, a code intended to unlock a phone requires an individualized access key per phone (using, e.g., the phone's unique identifier) and as many individual keys to be generated or retrieved as there are requests to unlock.[15]

Proponents and critics disagree about how much greater the risk of compromise would be as well as, at least implicitly, about how to weigh the incremental risk against the benefits of enabling government access.

How frequently might vendors be asked to unlock phones? It is difficult to predict the volume of requests to vendors, but a figure in the tens of thousands per year seems reasonable, given the number of criminal wiretaps per year in the United States and the number of inaccessible devices reported by just the FBI and the Manhattan District Attorney's Office (see the section "Encryption as an Impediment to Investigations" in Chapter 4). As a result, each vendor, depending on its market share, needs to be able to handle thousands to tens of thousands of domestic requests per year.

---

[15] S. Landau, 2017, "Punching the wrong bag: The deputy AG enters the crypto wars," *Lawfare Blog*, October 27, https://www.lawfareblog.com/punching-wrong-bag-deputy-ag-enters-crypto-wars.

Such a change in scale, as compared to the software update process, would necessitate a change in process and may require a larger number of people authorized to release an unlock code than are authorized to release a software update, which would increase the insider risk.

Critics worry that using this approach might erode trust in the software updates issued by vendors and lead users to eschew important security updates, thus significantly increasing their exposure to Internet malware and attacks by an array of actors. This risk stems in part from proponents having used software updates as an analogy to the unlocking process. If advocates of required vendor unlock were to avoid this analogy, that would reduce the level of mistrust. So, too, would avoiding requests that vendors subvert the software update process (as contrasted with implementing a per-device unlocking scheme) to unlock devices.

A related process and scale issue is the need for vendors to validate court documents before they release an unlock code or performing the unlock in order to thwart malevolent actors seeking to surreptitiously unlock devices. The challenge is similar to the one faced by telecommunications carriers with CALEA[16] or cloud providers served with requests for customer data. Such requirements could impose a burden on small vendors and constitute a barrier to entry for new vendors; small vendors would likely need to enlist trusted third parties similar to how telecommunications carriers ensure compliance with CALEA.

Whether or not this burden would be reasonable or not depends, of course, on how one weighs the innovation and public safety equities. Although, as occurs in other sectors, small businesses could be protected from a significant financial burden in response to a law enforcement request, this "solution" is only partially effective. Should a small vendor grow large—which can happen quickly for Internet applications—their system architecture must suddenly need to accommodate the assistance requirement. Thus a small vendor would essentially have to build provisions for exceptional access into their architecture from the outset. This may mean that both the financial burdens and security risks of the requirement are present even before the vendor is formally subject to it.

Requiring a U.S. vendor to have the ability to unlock every phone has the potential to erode trust in that vendor's products in the international market, but it is difficult to quantify the impact or assess how much additional impact the imposition of a U.S. requirement will have if other nations have already placed such requirements on a vendor. A competitor could argue that another vendor may cooperate with U.S. authorities

---

[16] Federal Communications Commission, *Second Report and Order and Memorandum in the Matter of Communications Assistance for Law Enforcement Act and Broadband Access and Services*, FCC 06-56, p. 11, https://apps.fcc.gov/edocs_public/attachmatch/FCC-06-56A1.pdf.

to unlock a foreign phone, even in circumstances where the government lacks the authority. (Of course even if the United States does not impose an access requirement, other countries certainly could as a condition of participating in their domestic markets.) Similarly, it would be unsettling if foreign vendors could unlock any phone belonging to U.S. individuals. In the hands of a foreign government, this capability could, for example, be used against a U.S. executive to undermine U.S. corporate secrets and national security.[17] The threat with respect to foreign governments is, of course, much lower in the case where the unlocking mechanism requires one to have physical possession of a device than in the case where a device can be unlocked remotely.

Key Escrow

Key escrow is a scheme where the keys needed to decrypt data are held in escrow—by the vendor, a third party, or the government—so that an authorized third party can access the keys. The key escrow approach is applicable both to data at rest and data in motion. When this approach was studied extensively in the 1990s, several specific proposals were made, and some products that implemented key escrow for encrypted network communications were built and offered commercially.

The escrowing party could be the government, or it could be some other entity or entities. If vendors hold the keys, then each vendor can choose its own algorithms and formats. If a U.S. agency is to hold the recovery key, there are two possibilities. One is that the government determines the algorithms and formats that vendors use when implementing key escrow. Another is that the vendor provides the government with the necessary code to hold escrowed keys and perform the unlocking. The former would impose additional burdens on the vendor to integrate the government's solution into its product or service (while also keeping it from selecting what it deems the best technical solution), while the latter would impose additional burdens on the government to maintain and operate a system for each product or service that it seeks to access. Note that the latter could also mean a similar situation that law enforcement currently faces with the complexity created by the plethora of changing formats, compression algorithms, and protocols used by software applications.

The use of a third party to escrow keys may be perceived as preferable to having government itself hold the keys, which may be an attractive alternative for vendors who do not want to manage keys and authenticate

---

[17] Of course the security risks to U.S. travelers are well known and assumed as a fact of life by many U.S. business travelers. Those handling sensitive information are generally advised to travel with a "throwaway" device to minimize their exposure.

requests for them, but third parties themselves will be attractive targets for attackers, especially if the same escrow agent maintains the keys for a wide range of systems.

One way to protect the key is to split it into pieces known as "shares" and store each share with a different organization. By analogy, many doors have a lower and upper lock for extra security. You could, of course, give the lower lock key to one friend and the upper lock key to another, making it hard for either friend to misuse your key and enter your home by his or herself. If you did it for the keys to an encrypted computer, it would mean that someone would need to attack both of your friends to unlock it. More complicated schemes allow the cryptographic key to be split—for example, into five shares so that any three can be used to decrypt. Two shares, however, are of no help in decrypting. Consequently, if two shares are compromised by an adversary, the data is still safe. This technique can be used to protect high-value secret keys. The proposals from the 1990s called for the law enforcement access secret keys to be split into parts held by separate government agencies. Although such a scheme provides additional security, it also introduces additional technical and organizational complexity to the key escrow system associated with retrieving and combining the shares and thus, potentially, creates additional risks.

The key escrow approaches that were proposed in the 1990s—and the Clipper proposal in particular—were reviewed extensively by independent researchers. Several weaknesses in Clipper that could interfere with government access were discovered,[18] but none were found that would weaken the encrypted communication between parties using the Clipper devices to communicate.

Owing to its complexity, it is difficult to design and implement a large-scale key escrow system securely. Indeed, a 1996 National Research Council report on cryptography[19] recommended that an escrow scheme be tested at scale before requiring its use, something that has never been done for an escrowed communications system.

That report did not study the then-proposed Clipper scheme in depth but found that any scheme that includes key escrow would result in enhanced law enforcement access to encrypted information but weaken the security of authorized users' information. The finding of weakened security was based on the theoretical potential for abuse or the potential for failure of the escrow mechanism. The report also found that there

---

[18] M. Blaze, 1994, "Protocol failure in the escrowed encryption standard," pp. 59-67 in *Proceedings of the 2nd ACM Conference on Computer and Communications Security*, Association of Computing Machinery, http://www.crypto.com/papers/eesproto.pdf.

[19] National Research Council, 1996, *Cryptography's Role in Securing the Information Society*, National Academy Press, Washington, D.C.

was some benefit to authorized users, especially of storage encryption systems, from an escrow mechanism that would allow users to recover their own stored data owing to a failure of the encryption system or associated key storage. The report made no attempt to quantify either benefit to law enforcement or cost in weakened security. Once the government abandoned its attempts to press for key escrow, Clipper and similar communications key escrow schemes disappeared from the market. There were few purchasers within the United States, and even fewer abroad.[20]

By contrast, many storage encryption products today offer key escrow-like features to avoid data loss or support business record management requirements. For example, Apple's full disk encryption for the Mac gives the user the option to, in effect, escrow the encryption key. Microsoft Windows' BitLocker feature escrows the key by default but allows users to request that the escrowed key be deleted. Some point to the existence of such products as evidence that key recovery for stored data can be implemented in a way that sensibly balances risks and benefits at least in certain contexts and against certain threats. In any case, data that is recoverable by a vendor without the user's passcode can be recovered by the vendor for law enforcement as well. Key escrow-type systems are especially prevalent and useful where the user, or some other authorized person such as the employer, needs access to stored data. Key escrow-type systems are less prevalent for transitory communications, including text messages, where the ability to retrieve past content is often less important. There are, however, some settings, such as the financial industry, where there are requirements that communications be stored and retrievable.

Hardware-Based Device-Level Key Escrow for Access to Stored Data

An alternative approach for access to mobile devices would be to escrow a device decryption key in the device itself—for example, by storing it in some form of secure hardware. To retrieve the key from the hardware module, an investigator would—after receiving proper legal authorization—be required to get an authentication token from the key holder. With this token, investigators would retrieve a key that can be used to decrypt the data stored on it. This would in turn require manufacturers to maintain a service to store and protect the keys used to generate the authentication tokens, validate law enforcement requests, and produce the tokens. This key could be stored whole or broken into pieces, with each piece escrowed separately with different parties. The

---

[20] W. Diffie and S. Landau, 2010, *Privacy on the Line: The Politics of Wiretapping and Encryption*, MIT Press, Cambridge, Mass.

mechanism for validating the authorization token and releasing the decryption key would be managed entirely by hardware and designed so that it could not be triggered by software running on the device. Compared to the key escrow option described above, this approach has the advantage of only allowing the decryption key to be retrieved if one has physical custody of the device, but, otherwise, it raises the same risks and complexities.

"Weaken" Encryption

There are several approaches to providing law enforcement access to encrypted information that fall into the general category of "weakening" encryption. One is to limit the key length so that law enforcement or intelligence agencies can reasonably recover plaintext by trying all possible keys. Another is to implement an encryption algorithm that incorporates a feature that allows authorized agencies to use a special key or algorithm to recover plaintext. The first alternative is very similar to the approach tried during the 1990s when exportable encryption products were limited to 40-bit keys. The second alternative, as described, has not previously been implemented although a variation of the first alternative, the IBM Commercial Data Masking Facility, involved manipulating a 56-bit DES key by setting certain bits to zero and encrypting the modified key using constant keys. Under that alternative, key management software continued to negotiate 56-bit keys, but law enforcement (or any other attacker) only had to exhaust a 40-bit key space to recover plaintext.

Both approaches to weakening encryption have generally fallen out of favor as possible solutions. With today's widespread availability of computing resources, many actors could exploit systems using shortened keys. Like any vulnerability, once discovered, such weaknesses can be exploited by anyone. And any solution that required shortened keys or use of a specific encryption method would create a legacy problem; systems would have to accommodate the shortened keys in protocols, even if the methodology were found to be insecure and abandoned. That would create long-term risks, not only to the systems that employed shortened keys, but also to all systems needing to interact with it.[21]

---

[21] The so-called FREAK exploit discovered in 2015 took advantage of flawed implementations of OpenSSL and Apple TLS/SSL client software. In unpatched systems, it allows an attacker to use a man-in-the-middle attack to force vulnerable clients and servers to use weakened encryption. See B. Beurdouche, K. Bhargavan, A. Delignat-Lavaud, C. Fournet, M. Kohlweiss, A. Pironti, P.-Y. Strub, and J.K. Zinzindohoue 2015, "A messy state of the union: Taming the composite state machines of TLS," pp. 535-552 in *2015 IEEE Symposium on Security and Privacy*, doi:10.1109/SP.2015.39.

Require Vendor Assistance But Impose
No Requirements on Deployed Technology

This variant of the above approaches would seek to compel vendors to render reasonable assistance on a case-by-case basis but not impose requirements on the technology they deploy to enable such assistance. It is an option that would presumably be pursued under the All Writs Act or some legislative clarification or extension of that law. Of course, there may be very different views as to what constitutes "reasonable"—both in terms of the costs to the vendor and the risks to a vendor (and its users) if the tool or technique used by the vendor is itself discovered or stolen and then exploited. This sort of divergence was on display in the San Bernardino case, where the FBI sought to have Apple prepare and sign software that would allow it to unlock a phone recovered from one of the shooters—a request that was withdrawn after the FBI found a third party that could unlock the phone. New legislation could help establish parameters for what is reasonable, but extensive litigation is likely. The effectiveness of this mechanism may erode as vendors improve security to respond to the general threat environment or—potentially—to specifically hamper such assistance.

It is also possible that the market will bifurcate. If the legal standard depends on the difficulty and cost of providing technical assistance, some companies will seek to raise those costs so as to not be required to provide such assistance. Alternatively, other companies will seek to make it as easy as possible to comply in order to keep costs down. One result would be that the accessibility of one's data by the government could vary quite a bit by vendor.

Future Cryptographic Technologies

New cryptographic techniques might change the parameters of the debate in the future. Standard encryption enables anyone who holds the secret key to fully decrypt, while all others learn nothing about the plaintext data. Modern cryptography now offers a richer set of capabilities than simply full access or no access. For example, when certain ciphers are used to encrypt, it is possible to issue a *restricted* secret key that lets the key holder ascertain whether a certain keyword or phrase appears in the plaintext but learn nothing else about the plaintext. In theory, this restricted key could enable law enforcement to determine whether a suspected device contained certain keywords or phrases, while learning nothing else about the contents of the device. Researchers continue to make advances in this general technical area, but technologies for a general-purpose search on encrypted data are not yet ready for mass adoption.

These techniques would also pose many challenges in the context of investigations. First, even simple obfuscation, such as avoiding likely key words or obfuscating the text by replacing the letter "i" with the letter "l" (ell) will prevent a keyword match. More aggressive text obfuscation—notably prior encryption using other cryptography—will prevent the search from working altogether. Finally, a scheme that uses a restricted secret key generated by a trusted authority has the same difficulties as the key escrow schemes discussed above.

Ways to Bypass a Plaintext Access Mandate

In the 1990s, law enforcement authorities seemed willing to accept the risk that end-users would install encryption features that did not implement the (then-proposed) key escrow mechanisms. Today, a similar question about effectiveness arises with proposals to regulate the use of encryption in mass-market products and services. Sophisticated criminals have always had means to evade surveillance, while changing the defaults has the potential to affect a much wider range of investigations. Nevertheless it is important to note that smart and determined actors can employ a variety of techniques that can be used to evade a mandate against default encryption. At the same time, most people accept vendor defaults, even when they may present risks to their security and privacy. The discussion below does not speak to *whether* bad actors will seek to circumvent regulations on encryption but rather *how* they might go about doing so.

A few possible techniques are discussed below.

Adapt to a Platform-Level Mandate by Adopting Application-Level Encryption

If cryptography is implemented inside an application, a mandate placed on the vendor's hardware and operating system (such as an Apple iPhone and its operating system iOS or the multiple vendors of Android phones) will not provide access to that application's data, because even once the phone's disk is decrypted, the application's data remains encrypted and unavailable to an investigator. Already, dozens of applications support such application-level encryption, and many are developed outside of the United States. These include stand-alone applications that would allow a user to store encrypted files on a smart phone or laptop. Of course, if the user chooses a weak password in the application or a flaw in the application can be identified and exploited, it may still be possible to gain access.

One could imagine imposing a similar requirement on all application developers, but there are a number of complications. First, developers reside worldwide, and it is not clear how one would impose this mandate on everyone. In fact, as with mandated access to devices, this mandate could disadvantage U.S. developers relative to foreign developers who are not subject to the mandate. Second, as in the case of mandated vendor unlock, discussed above, it raises scale and process challenges for small firms. Third, even if one can regulate application software produced by companies, there is a wide range of open-source software with encryption capabilities that is freely available and modifiable.[22]

With some platforms, such as Apple's iPhone, only applications approved by the vendor can be installed through the normal software installation channel. On these platforms, it may be possible to block the installation of applications that provide unapproved encryption.[23] However, there are several ways for a determined and knowledgeable user to bypass these restrictions.

On some platforms, applications can be loaded from any number of widely available application stores. Even on more restricted platforms, such as Apple's iPhone, applications can be "side loaded" using freely available developer tools and distributed on a limited basis by anyone with a developer account. Another possibility is to "jailbreak" the phone (see below) and disable or remove the offending features.[24] Moreover, platforms such as Android and iOS provide at least a limited ability for running code entered by the user. For example, one can install a Python interpreter from Apple's app store that can access the system clipboard, and use it for encryption and decryption.

Applications providing encryption could even be run entirely within a Web browser, making it even more difficult to regulate their use. As with jailbreaking (see below), it is important to understand how much such bypassing erodes the benefits to law enforcement of access mandates. There are also platforms, such as the open-source Android operating system, that do not impose such restrictions on what software can be installed.

These considerations point to the difference between an exceptional access regime intended to work against a skillful adversary, which is impractical, and making it work for mass-market, default communications and storage products and services. The only way to guarantee that

---

[22] A recent global survey of encryption products found that one-third were open source. See B. Schneier, K. Seidel, and S. Vijayakumar, 2016, *A Worldwide Survey of Encryption Products*, Berkman Center Research Publication No. 2016-2, https://ssrn.com/abstract=2731160.

[23] Indeed, Apple recently removed encryption and VPN software from its China app store at the request of the Chinese government.

[24] Because jailbreaking involves breaking the secure boot mechanism, it reduces protection against malicious software.

every form of encryption is subject to exceptional access is to certify the software that is allowed to run on every storage and communication device, which would be extremely expensive, intrusive, and bad for innovation. Consider by analogy the situation with physical search: a skillful adversary can make it effectively impossible for government to find physical objects, but it is tricky, expensive, and inconvenient to do this, so one does not abandon physical search just because it may not be effective in some circumstances.

Also, with respect to the possibility that third parties create applications that provide encryption without exceptional access, it is important to bear in mind that correctly designing and implementing systems that use encryption is challenging. One consequence in a world in which exceptional access is mandated is that systems without exceptional access may be less secure than mainstream systems that do provide exceptional access. The latter can benefit from the resources and expertise of the large enterprises or consortia that develop, deploy, and maintain them, which may stand in contrast to the groups that build capabilities intended to thwart a requirement.[25]

Install Alternative Operating System Software

Vendor mandates rely on devices running operating system software that properly responds to unlock codes. If the user is able to alter the existing operating system or install an alternative operating system (which on some platforms requires circumventing vendor security measures), the device may no longer respond to unlock codes. When faced with such a device, law enforcement might be unable to unlock it, even with the vendor's assistance.

Jailbreaking of mobile devices is a fairly common occurrence, although by no means universal—and vendors are strongly motivated to prevent all devices they have supplied from being broken by a single "wholesale" attack of the sort needed for a jailbreak. It is worth noting that an exploit used to jailbreak is different from one that is used to circumvent a device lock and encryption; jailbreaks work only after a phone has been unlocked.

---

[25] Note, however, that the messaging app Signal, which is believed to work securely, was developed by two people. A system that includes exceptional access would be more complicated and might require a larger team.

Use Legacy Devices or Software

This technique relies on continuing to use devices or software that are not compliant with a new regulation. It is in general difficult to stop people from using old hardware and software, although this is a time-bounded problem as people upgrade to take advantage of new capabilities. As discussed above, app store restrictions do not apply on all platforms and, in any event, are not foolproof for restricting access to non-compliant software. With respect to hardware, legacy smartphones could presumably be restricted through regulations on what devices cellular carriers allow to connect to their networks, but laptops and other hardware could not similarly be regulated.

Use Other Techniques for Concealing Messages and Stored Data

Finally, determined actors can use other techniques to conceal messages or stored data. One way is to use steganography, a technique where one hides private information by embedding it in public data. For example, one can hide secret information in public images such as pictures of cats. The information is hidden in the pixels representing the cats. Only someone who knows where to look will find the data. To a law enforcement agent, the images look like normal uninteresting images. Many free steganography applications are currently available for both Android and iOS, and all are quite easy to install and use. The use of such applications could be regulated, subject to all of the caveats as for encryption applications. It is sometimes possible to detect but not necessarily to decrypt steganographic messages.

Another technique is to employ secret sharing, where the user splits a file into two or more shares, where a single share reveals nothing about the file contents. Each share is stored on a different device, so that capture of a single device reveals nothing. An investigator who recovers a phone but not the other device will learn little from unlocking it.

Alternatives to Exceptional Access

There are other avenues for investigators to gain access to plaintext and other digital information that may aid an investigation. Some have argued that these tools, especially in aggregate, may serve as at least a partial substitute for regulations that mandate exceptional access. Others, notably from the law enforcement community, have warned that these tools, although useful in some cases, will not be a satisfactory substitute in many others. The following are some important examples.

Use Metadata

Although encryption hides content, current encryption systems generally do not hide metadata. For example, in a chat system, metadata includes information such as who communicated with whom, for how long, the participant's location, and so on. Metadata is also needed to prevent spamming and denial of service, which is why many existing systems collect this information. Such metadata provides new sources of information not previously available to investigators that exceeds the old "who called whom when" provided by the telephone network.[26] Nonetheless, metadata is not necessarily a substitute for content (see the section "The Practical Utility of Alternatives to Exceptional Access" in Chapter 4). It is not a given that all metadata will remain unencrypted. Methods have been developed for hiding "who communicated with whom." As these technologies become more robust and popular, even some basic metadata could become unavailable.

Access Data Stored in Cloud Services

In coming years, the majority of user data at rest will probably be stored in the cloud. Because in many instances users or service providers want access to this data (e.g., for searching, aggregation, and analysis), the data is typically stored in a way that enables the provider to access the data in the clear. Law enforcement can interact with cloud providers to obtain data that they need for investigations, such as data mirrored or backed up from mobile devices. Using this approach requires no modification of cryptographic systems on the mobile devices. However, some firms offer services that encrypt data so that the service provider cannot access it. Also, users who are sensitive to the possibility of government access can generally opt out of cloud storage for their data.

Lawful Hacking

This section focuses on technical aspects of lawful hacking; legal aspects are discussed in the section "Legal Aspects of Lawful Hacking" above.

The scope of impact—and potential risk—will depend on the exploit that is used. Sometimes the government will succeed through an approach that affects only a single device, such as leveraging misconfigurations of a target system. Other times, the government will exploit a vulnerability in

---

[26] Berkman Center for Internet and Society at Harvard University, 2016, *Don't Panic: Making Progress on the "Going Dark" Debate*, February 1, https://cyber.harvard.edu/pubrelease/dont-panic/Dont_Panic_Making_Progress_on_Going_Dark_Debate.pdf.

the target system. When the government finds vulnerabilities in products that lead to exploits, it can choose to either collect these exploits or report the vulnerabilities to the vendor. The product is vulnerable in either case; choosing which alternative to take is a matter of policy. But the fact that the vulnerability was discovered means it is possible that others will discover it too, although the probability of independent discovery is a matter of debate.

The equities for lawful hacking may vary considerably depending on the particular circumstances. For example, one consequence of pursuing this approach is that it increases the incentives for government (and the contractors that provide lawful hacking services to government) to acquire and hold exploits rather than report them to vendors. As with the use of hacking techniques for foreign intelligence collection, it requires that the benefits to investigators be balanced with the risks to users of systems with unpatched vulnerabilities. The Obama administration established the "vulnerabilities equities process" in an attempt to address these trade-offs, and it has recently been updated and made public.[27] Another consideration with respect to equities is that vulnerabilities are fragile; they may be discovered and fixed if they are used. They may also be discovered and reused by other parties. A final risk is that information about vulnerabilities or hacking tools that use them can leak or be stolen from government agencies and then be used by malicious actors.

From a technical perspective, there are three domains where tools are needed: locked devices, encrypted data in the cloud, and encrypted communications. In each case, the challenge for investigators is acquiring the tools needed to cover all the devices and services that may arise in investigations—and obtaining the necessary resources. For which devices would law enforcement have hacking tools, and would those tools require physical possession of the device? Another is the time and effort required to use the tools. From the perspective of law enforcement, something fast and reliable would be best, but one can imagine tools that require thousands of dollars' worth of computation or days to weeks of effort. Moreover, given the fragility and specificity of lawful hacking approaches, law enforcement will need to develop or otherwise acquire a large number of exploits, which will be expensive and time-consuming. Such delay may be acceptable for some investigations, but for others, it may put law enforcement into a situation where they are always lagging the events they are charged to investigate.

Exploitable vulnerabilities will always be present in software, espe-

---

[27] Executive Office of the President, 2017, *Vulnerabilities Equities Policy and Process for the United States Government*, November 15, https://www.whitehouse.gov/sites/whitehouse.gov/files/images/External%20-%20Unclassified%20VEP%20Charter%20FINAL.PDF.

cially in large and complex systems. However, it will not necessarily be easy for the government, especially state and local law enforcement agencies, to stay ahead of continually improving security technologies. Many vendors have made major investments in software security, which will likely raise the cost of discovering vulnerabilities. Patches are also available much more rapidly in today's environment where users are accustomed to constant updates. Trusted boot, which is fundamental to device encryption, has made malware implantation harder. Other security advances that impede hackers include anti-hammering protections (which mitigate the risk of repetitive password attacks), biometric and two-factor authentication (which reduces reliance on passwords and the risk of phishing), and anonymous routing services (which makes it more difficult to identify endpoints and targets). Additionally, if the lawful hacking attack is discovered and the attack vector is understood and publicized, it will be remediated, creating further challenges for those seeking access—assuming the software is updated, which may or may not be automatic depending on the particular vendor and context.

As a result, lawful hacking of individual communications applications such as Snapchat and devices such as iPhones and laptops with full disk encryption will require a level of effort that may well not scale to the number of investigations implicated and may well not be feasible for all investigative agencies. There are also limits on what tools may be appropriate for law enforcement agencies to use. For example, some of the means at the disposal of the National Security Agency would be inappropriate or illegal for traditional law enforcement.

Acquire Better Tools and Capabilities for Accessing and Analyzing Plaintext

As observed earlier, encryption is not the only barrier to effective use of plaintext. Even when information is not encrypted, it can be difficult for law enforcement or intelligence agencies to access and analyze information. Information may be transmitted using nonstandard protocols or stored in unfamiliar formats—and these may change on a regular basis as companies evolve software and services. Making effective use of data, especially when the volumes are large, requires specialized tools and expertise. Acquiring these capabilities will require additional resources; see the next section.

ENHANCED FINANCIAL AND TECHNICAL SUPPORT

The following are options for providing additional financial or technical support to respond to the challenges posed by encryption:

- *Provide law enforcement with additional financial resources.* Law enforcement capabilities and spending have not kept pace with the growing role of digital evidence in investigations.[28] In today's world of multiple types of devices, applications, and networks, the "one-size-fits-all" solutions of the telephony era are no longer possible. Thus greater technical expertise is a necessity in modern investigations. With additional resources, the government could hire more specialists, pursue more sources of information, find additional clever workarounds when data is encrypted, expand capabilities for lawful hacking, and find and punish more criminals. As indicated previously, with more resources, law enforcement would be able to access and use sources of information that are now too difficult.
- *Sharing and access to specialized services.* When one law enforcement group learns how to use a new source of data, or finds (or develops) a useful tool, how do other law enforcement groups learn about this, as there are surely some that could use it? More broadly, there are clear economies of scale. A small town—or even small city—police department cannot maintain the technical staff needed to find new sources of data or learn about new methods and tools. At the same time, it may be desirable to limit the spread of sensitive techniques used to access plaintext, lest they leak out and bad actors either learn how to circumvent them or make use of the techniques for their own purposes.

Both formal and informal sharing institutions can play a role if properly staffed and funded. Existing specialized federal entities and government-affiliated nonprofits (Box 5.2) and the existing analysis capabilities of federal, state, and local law enforcement agencies can be leveraged to assist law enforcement groups that lack the necessary skills and equipment. For this assistance to partially offset the loss of plaintext, the capabilities and scale of these entities may well have to increase by orders of magnitude.

- *Enhance corporate outreach to law enforcement.* Companies could enhance their efforts to engage the law enforcement community, making sure law enforcement officials are familiar with their products and what data does and does not exist. (Fully implementing this would require a detailed discussion of the changing details of what data is retained, how its location is determined, and how long it is kept.) The U.S. Department

---

[28] The gap is recognized in the FBI's fiscal year (FY) 2017 budget request that included an increase of $38 million to "counter the threat of Going Dark" (U.S. Department of Justice, FY 2017 Authorization and Budget Request to Congress, https://www.justice.gov/jmd/file/821341/download). The FY2018 request calls for an increase of $22 million, 80 positions, and 20 agents for "Going Dark/Investigative Technology"(U.S. Department of Justice, FY 2018 Budget Request at a Glance, https://www.justice.gov/jmd/page/file/968261/download).

> **BOX 5.2**
> **Technical Assistance and Training Organizations**
>
> **Federal Government Organizations**
>
> • The National Domestic Communications Assistance Center, a center organized under the U.S. Department of Justice, provides state and local law enforcement investigators with access to subject matter experts and technical tools and services. It also provides training on new and emerging technologies, industry processes, and how to develop tools for interpreting digital evidence.
> • The Federal Law Enforcement Training Centers, a program of the U.S. Department of Homeland Security, provide training to law enforcement on a wide array of topics including digital evidence acquisition and forensics, evidence recovery from seized computers, and Internet investigations.
> • The National Computer Forensics Institute, operated by the U.S. Secret Service, provides state and local law enforcement with training in digital evidence and cyber crime investigations.
>
> **Nonprofits**
>
> • The National Consortium for Justice Information and Statistics Assistance and Training Center offers training on investigating digital crimes and working with digital evidence.
> • The National Center for Missing and Exploited Children provides online and classroom training on forensic imaging and other skills needed to investigate cases of missing and sexually exploited children.
> • The National White Collar Crime Center provides information and training on investigative techniques, tools, and best practices related to cyber and economic crime.
> • The National Criminal Justice Training Center of Fox Valley Technical College provides training on digital investigations and technology-facilitated crimes against children.

of Justice's National Domestic Communications Assistance Center currently facilitates some level of assistance. Other avenues for cooperation include the following:

— *Vendors supply source code and internal documentation.* Some vendors, such as those selling secure messaging, might be willing to voluntarily supply information if the government's equities process provides sufficient priority to the release of vulnerabilities to vendors so that the vendors can remediate them. One objection is that for many programs the implementation changes several times a year, so guaranteeing that the supplied code is what is running on a particular device would be challenging. In the long run, this is likely to make the systems more secure; law enforcement's opportunity comes between the discovery of an exploitable vulnerability and when it is patched in the systems they care about. Pursuing this option assumes that the vulnerabilities equities process favors disclosure to the vendor and assumes that law enforcement agencies have the capability to discover new vulnerabilities.

— *Vendors voluntarily share information about vulnerabilities.* Vendors will fix the security vulnerabilities they find, but in the interim, legitimate government interests as well as bad actors could potentially make use of the vulnerabilities. Absent a requirement to share these bugs, it is not clear, especially in the current environment, whether vendors would actually participate; they generally avoid sharing vulnerabilities for any offensive purpose in part because they fear legal liability and reputational damage if they enable their own customers to be attacked successfully. With both this case and the one that follows, a further complication to consider is the risk that the government agencies that hold a vulnerability may lose it; the risk is more than theoretical in light of reports about government-held tools being compromised.

— *Third parties voluntarily share information about vulnerabilities.* Third parties often discover security vulnerabilities and report them to vendors. They could share this information to the government before or at the same time they provide it to vendors.

- *Support innovation.* Research funding may lead to innovative technical solutions that better accommodate government access and end-user security. One example would be searchable encryption, discussed above as well as in Chapter 2.

LEGISLATION MANDATING ACCESS

As discussed earlier, there are two broad categories of possible legislation mandating government access to encrypted information.

- *Enact legislation that requires that device vendors or service providers provide government access to plaintext without specifying the technical means of doing so.* The mandate could be described in a variety of ways, with different types of problems. For example, it might require that vendors be able to comply with warrants seeking access to the plaintext of the information when their products and services are used to encrypt but leave it to industry to design the technical solution.
- *Enact legislation requiring a particular technical approach.* For example, a law or regulation could require vendors to implement hardware-based device-level key escrow for access to stored data or require vendors or third-party key escrow for access to communications. As a middle ground, a law could call for rulemaking to select a technical approach.

The first approach has the advantage of allowing industry greater flexibility in developing and selecting solutions that best fit their technical and business circumstances. On the other hand, if industry is left to choose, there may be a plethora of plaintext recovery solutions adopted. This cacophony in the marketplace may be a challenge to government agents, because they will have to rely on different techniques in different cases. But because the United States cannot regulate what applications and devices are developed outside U.S. borders, some degree of cacophony is likely to exist for investigators regardless of limits created by U.S. legislation.

By contrast, the second approach may be more burdensome if the selected approach is difficult for vendors to implement, and it would not foster innovative solutions. However, it may provide the greatest scale because law enforcement would have a repeatable and dependable way to access plaintext when authorized pursuant to law. By having everyone adopt the same technical approach, it would also magnify the risk of catastrophic failure if that common approach were to have exploitable security flaws.

Even for a technically non-specific mandate, there are many details that would need to be worked out and specified in a legislative proposal. For example,

- Which companies, products, and services are covered, and what are the exact responsibilities of vendors and service providers?
- How will legacy devices be treated? Are they exempt from the requirements, or must they be taken out of service if they cannot comply? If they are not grandfathered, how will the requirements be enforced?
- How robust must the exceptional access mechanism be against user efforts to disable it?
- What rules apply to devices that are carried into the United States by foreign visitors? Must they be retrofitted or disabled at the border? Similarly, what rules apply to services provided by firms without a clear U.S. presence, and how would these rules be enforced?

In terms of cost, if industry is left to innovate, it will incur research and development costs, product (re)development costs, and the costs of adhering with any access regime. (Some of those costs are incurred today with regard to access to plaintext, such as the costs of responding to judicial process.) If the government mandates a particular solution, there will be the cost of re-engineering systems, protecting the access mechanisms, and responding to government requests for data.

6

International Dimensions

Encryption is a global issue for nations, corporations, and individuals. However, as characterized by a recent Center for Strategic and International Studies report,[1] despite "global concern" there is no "global consensus." Although the debate on encryption continues, a clear trend is the increasing demands of governments for access to data from Internet companies as recorded by "transparency reports" whether by domestic U.S. legal process or foreign requests.[2] A number of countries are currently exploring a variety of regulatory approaches, with significant variation even within the European Union.[3,4]

There are several concurrent themes to the international dimensions of the issue.

- *Global availability.* Because encryption technologies are available and developed globally, there are limits to what can be achieved with domestic regulation.

---

[1] J.A. Lewis, D.E. Zheng, and W.A. Carter, 2017, *Effect of Encryption of Lawful Access to Communications and Data: A Report of the CSIS Technology Policy Program*, https://www.csis.org/analysis/effect-encryption-lawful-access-communications-and-data.

[2] "Hand Over the Data," 2017, *Technology Review* 102(2):26.

[3] D. Severson, n.d., *The Encryption Debate in Europe*, Aegis Paper Series No. 1702, research report, Hoover Institution, http://www.hoover.org/sites/default/files/research/docs/severson_webreadypdf.pdf.

[4] S. Herpig and S. Heuman, 2017, "Germany's crypto past and hacking future," *Lawfare Blog* (April 13), https://www.lawfareblog.com/germanys-crypto-past-and-hacking-future.

- *Potential proliferation of national regulation.* Other nations are already seeking to regulate encryption and impose access requirements. Those measures may affect the United States in various ways. At the same time, if the U.S. government takes steps to mandate companies to provide access to encrypted content, it will encourage other countries to demand access as well. The resulting proliferation of approaches to enforce such an access requirement may give rise to a patchwork multinational regulatory structure that will likely decrease the technology products that can be sold to the global market.
- *Restrictions on international data transfer.* Given the amount of Internet traffic that transits the United States and the amount of data stored by U.S. technology companies, any movement toward legislated access for the U.S. government will create concern by other countries that the United States does not have adequate controls over whether law enforcement and/or the intelligence community are accessing the data of citizens of their country. This dynamic may put international data transfer mechanisms, such as the EU-U.S. Privacy Shield Framework, at risk of further legal and political challenges, especially in the European Union. Weakening the mechanisms that allow for lawful international data transfer to the United States will create a disincentive to use U.S. technology and communications networks.
- *Global impacts of domestic regulations on citizens of other nations.* Citizens around the world have become more aware of and sometimes concerned about the possibility of surveillance by nations other than their own.

Decisions on encryption will have critical consequences for international trade and the competitiveness of U.S. companies whether or not the approaches and solutions are adopted worldwide (and they seem unlikely to be). Any government decisions requiring exceptional access, whether in the United States or elsewhere, are also likely to have global ramifications for human rights, especially privacy, freedoms of speech and association, and the right to information (see Chapter 3). Corporations are faced with the choice of complying with country-specific laws or foregoing markets for their products. As outlined in Chapter 5, countries have a variety of options for responding to the encryption dilemma.

Vendors, whether based in the United State or elsewhere, generally rely on complex international supply chains for the hardware and software that comprise their products and services. This dependence creates opportunities for coercion by foreign governments.

Another international issue is the Mutual Legal Assistance Treaty (MLAT) process through which a country may seek data that is held in another country. This is related to the encryption debate because one approach when encryption is encountered in an investigation is to seek alternative sources of data stored in the cloud. Increasingly, that data may turn out to be stored in another country, which under the existing process greatly complicates and delays access. Numerous studies have called for reform to enhance both the speed and process to ensure better effectiveness but the framework relies on voluntary cooperation. There are already efforts in this direction, such as those between the United States and United Kingdom. Civil liberties and human rights organizations have expressed concerns that current proposals do not incorporate adequate safeguards to protect individual rights. It may be that international agreements will be easiest in the context of responding to specific types of crimes, such as terrorism or child exploitation. Similarly, it will be much easier to reach bilateral or multilateral agreements regarding law enforcement interests than intelligence interests.

EFFECTS OF U.S. ACTIONS ON OTHER COUNTRIES AND THE INTERNATIONAL MARKET FOR U.S. GOODS AND SERVICES

For U.S. vendors, a mandate to provide access could have a significant impact on global revenue. For most multi-national companies, a significant portion of their revenue is generated overseas, owing to demographics (e.g., China and India have more than 1 billion people each) and large potential opportunities in emerging markets more broadly. At the same time, some of the customers in these jurisdictions may be reluctant to use products that provide government access to plaintext, particularly U.S. government access to plaintext. The impact will be sensitive to the particular technical approach used. For example, if key escrow were implemented but the keys were to be stored only in the country of the customer, some customers might find that approach acceptable because they are already subject to local laws. It seems plausible that whether they do will depend on whether the country in question provides strong rule-of-law protections; customers may nevertheless be concerned about U.S. firms providing data to the U.S. government. At the same time, some customers in some markets may be more affected by their own country's approach to encryption than by the U.S. approach, even if they are buying products from U.S. companies. Indeed, in some cases U.S. firms have tailored their products and services to the regulations of a country in order to participate in that market.[5] On the other hand, an approach that uses local stor-

---

[5] See, for example, P. Mozur, 2017, "Apple removes apps from China store that help internet users evade censorship," *New York Times*, July 29, https://www.nytimes.com/2017/07/29/technology/china-apple-censorhip.html.

age of escrowed keys and gives repressive regimes control over those keys might not be supported by the United States as an international solution.

The international challenges are compounded by the fact that mobile devices are mobile, which means that a solution does not necessarily satisfy law enforcement needs; for example, sophisticated criminals could simply purchase devices outside the nation in which they intend to use them. Further compounding the challenge is the intersection of encryption and trade policy. For example, trade agreements may constrain how the U.S. government treats foreign visitor's devices that do not comply with U.S. rules.

The market for encryption products is a global market. It has been estimated that as of early 2016 there are 846 encryption products on the market of which 545 are produced outside of the United States.[6] Requirements for government exceptional access in U.S. encryption products, may drive people toward products designed in countries without any encryption regulation. Such a dynamic would, if it plays out in this way, weaken the competitiveness of U.S. companies while reducing the benefits for law enforcement.

GLOBAL NORMS

The challenges of addressing government exceptional access internationally stem in part from the lack of global norms around such related issues as security interests, business-government relationships, and information and communications privacy. Although the United Nations Group of Government Experts on Developments in the Field of Information and Telecommunications in the Context of International Security (UNGGE) has been meeting since 2010, there has been little success in establishing norms and confidence-building measures for responsible behavior and the application of international law. To be sure, a set of principles has been promulgated, but the insight from two decades ago by another National Research Council study still remains true today—international communications are conducted with no universally adopted information or communications privacy and security standards or policies.[7] The historical experience suggests that it will be difficult to reach agreement on international norms for exceptional access.

There have been a number of (to date unsuccessful) private-sector initiatives to establish industry norms and advocate that states create

---

[6] B. Schneier, K. Seidel, and S. Vijayakumar, 2016, "A Worldwide Survey of Encryption Products," Berkman Center Research Publication No. 2016-2, https://ssrn.com/abstract=2731160. Note that not all of the products listed in this survey are complete solutions, provide robust security, or are easy to use.

[7] National Research Council, 1996, *Cryptography's Role in Securing the Information Society*, National Academy Press, Washington DC.

both offensive and defensive norms to foster and maintain trust in mass-market products and services. As part of these appeals industry has requested the establishment of principle-based and coordinated policies on how to handle vulnerabilities. The plan for implementation would be to use intergovernmental forums—such as the G20, Global Conferences on Cyberspace, Organization for Security and Cooperation in Europe (OSCE), Shanghai Cooperative Organization (SCO), UNGGE, or the U.N. Institute for Disarmament Research—to establish this framework.[8] Multi-stakeholder forums such as the recently established Global Commission on the Stability of Cyberspace, which seeks to develop norms to enhance peace and security in cyberspace, may also offer another avenue for seeking consensus.

However, the differing expectations in areas such as business-government relationships, fair "business practices," and the role of major power security interests plague the possibility of solutions. The prerequisite for a global information structure remains the same—national governments must agree to the principles. This prerequisite remains the answer and the problem.

For products and services that provide encryption, one could try to establish an international uniform model code, a harmonization of the laws, increased mutual recognition of products, or some international interoperability regime for encryption. Each solution has its advantages—however, unless a strategic approach is taken, the global market on encryption may fragment with more authoritarian nation-states mandating access and the market producing inaccessible products for individuals willing to take the risk to secure communications and suffer the state consequences. At the same time, an effort to reach agreement on standards might not provide the level of protection for privacy and civil liberties that some nations or other stakeholders might expect or require.

In short, a global solution seems unlikely and the governments of the United States and other countries and the vendors based in or doing business in these countries will be faced with difficult trade-offs. Key questions include how the U.S. government and others decide to proceed domestically and internationally, and how these government decisions affect the trade-offs made by vendors.

---

[8] S. Charney et al., 2016, "From Articulation to Implementation: Enabling Progress on Cybersecurity Norms," Microsoft Corporation, https://mscorpmedia.azureedge.net/mscorpmedia/2016/06/Microsoft-Cybersecurity-Norms_vFinal.pdf.

7

A Framework for Evaluating Approaches to Access Plaintext

As discussed earlier, prominent leaders of the law enforcement community have warned that encryption is restricting their access to unencrypted stored data or message plaintext and that even as the volume of digital information expands, important parts of the digital world are "going dark" as more stored data and communications are encrypted by default. Some members of the intelligence community have concurred that pieces of the digital world are getting "dimmer" although not necessarily "dark." Thus, some government officials have argued that they need a reliable, timely, and scalable way to access plaintext. They point to (1) the widespread and increasing use of encryption by default in widely used products and services, (2) the myriad national security threats posed by terrorist groups and foreign rivals, (3) the increasing importance of digital evidence as human activity and crime have become increasingly digital, and (4) the limited effectiveness of alternative sources of digital evidence.

Opponents of regulations that would afford government exceptional access to plaintext have objected on a number of legal and practical grounds. Their primary arguments are that any regime by which providers of products and services featuring encryption are required to provide a way for ensuring government access to plaintext likely would (1) be ineffective, (2) pose unacceptable risks to cybersecurity, (3) pose unacceptable risks to privacy and civil liberties, (4) disadvantage U.S. providers of products and services, and (5) hamper innovation in encryption technologies. They take the view that the growing use of information technology and sophisticated collection and analysis capabilities have created a wealth of information for investigators.

With arguments on both sides, how can policymakers and citizens decide what to do? How can they evaluate the policy choices of whether to enable law enforcement and the intelligence community to maintain their current level of access, provide more resources to facilitate lawful government access, impose a legal requirement for mandatory access, or pursue other options? How can they assess the effect of each approach on law enforcement and national security, computer and data security, privacy and civil liberties, competitiveness, and other important values?

To inform that evaluation, this chapter provides a framework of questions that the committee believes any proposal must address. It captures the issues that the committee grappled with as it considered potential approaches and the broader context in which they arise. The objective of this framework is not simply to help policymakers determine whether a particular approach is optimal or desirable, but also to help ensure that any approach that policymakers might pursue is implemented in a way that maximizes its effectiveness while minimizing harmful side effects.

Importantly, in addressing these questions, policymakers will have to contend with incomplete data, limits on the ability to measure important properties, and an inability to fully predict the consequences of courses of action (Box 7.1). They will also need to contend with the complexity introduced by the thousands of communications and computing products available today, an international marketplace where new computing and communications products and services are introduced with regularity, and the interactions of those markets with the strategies and policies that are adopted by other nations.

Underlying the questions are a set of trade-offs associated with encryption and government access. One of the fundamental trade-offs is

---

BOX 7.1
Data Limitations and Uncertainties

• *Incomplete data on the impacts on law enforcement.* The Federal Bureau of Investigation and some jurisdictions have provided figures for a growing number of phones they cannot unlock, but the data—especially at the state and local level—are incomplete, and this data does not tell us how often investigations and prosecutions are thwarted. It is difficult in practice to collect systematic or comprehensive data: it is time consuming; assessments of impact are inherently

continued

BOX 7.1 Continued

subjective; data sources are highly distributed; and there is no infrastructure in place for collection or reporting, especially at the state and local levels. Relatedly, although there is some information about default use of encryption based on its availability in major platforms, there is little data on either deliberate use of encryption by either average citizens or criminals.

- *Limited ability to measure security risks.* One of the arguments against adding exceptional access features to encryption systems is that it adds risk when computer systems are already at great risk and that the added risk is unacceptable. The incremental risk of any proposed scheme is quite difficult to quantify, however, given the general difficulty in measuring the security of any computer system.
- *Difficulty partitioning consumer and business services.* One might seek to regulate encryption used for consumer services such as messaging but not business services where the added security risks might outweigh the benefits for law enforcement investigations. However, such efforts to partition the problem must take into account the considerable use of consumer services in enterprise settings. For example, "bring your own device" smartphones may be used to authenticate users for sensitive corporate applications. At the same time, unlike in the consumer market, access mechanisms are generally required in business settings for recovery or regulatory compliance.
- *Technology changes by vendors.* One of the alternatives to exceptional access to smartphones is for investigators to obtain cloud backups of phone data. That option would be blocked if vendors were to move either by default or as an option to user-controlled encryption. Similarly, vendors decisions to encrypt metadata would change its availability to investigators.
- *Necessarily speculative projections about future behavior.* There are also a number of cases where one can only speculate about future behaviors that have bearing on the implications of government regulation of encryption. For example, if the government were to require vendors to provide exceptional access, the effectiveness of that measure would depend in part on how many and which users chose to install alternative applications that do not afford exceptional access. Those who have objected to proposals to require key escrow observe that criminals will simply download noncompliant, unbreakable encryption software, which is widely available globally. On the other hand, most users tend to accept product defaults. What percentage of criminals will actually take the extra step to install and use noncompliant software? Clearly, the answer is greater than 0 percent (some will) but less than 100 percent (some will not). Similarly, some have argued that non-U.S. business customers will be reluctant to buy products whose encryption keys are accessible to the U.S. government. That may be true, too, but some multinational business have a U.S. presence and can be compelled to produce plaintext data anyway, while others may store their data out of the reach of the United States (i.e., the U.S. government might be able to compel the production of the key, but it would have no data to decrypt). So what percentage of foreign companies will actually eschew U.S. products because key recovery has been mandated? Again, the answer lies between 0 and 100 percent. In short, with quantification so difficult, it is difficult to assess the trade-offs and difficult to predict, in advance, how any proposed approach will work in practice.

that adding exceptional access capability to encryption schemes necessarily weakens their security to some degree, while the absence of an exceptional access mechanism necessarily hampers government investigations to some degree (Box 7.2). If the extent of those impacts were clear and could be weighed, it would certainly help illuminate the path forward, but, alas, the impacts are not precisely quantifiable. As the debate proceeds, it will help to have a framework to sort through the issues.

**BOX 7.2
A Fundamental Trade-Off**

There is a fundamental trade-off associated with providing the government with exceptional access to devices and services that use encryption to protect the confidentiality of communications or stored data or to lock devices. Exceptional access necessarily weakens security to some degree, while the absence of exceptional access necessarily hampers government investigations to some degree.

- *Impact on security.* Exceptional access features, no matter how well designed and implemented, will reduce their security to some degree as a result of the added complexity and greater potential for weaknesses in their design, implementation, or operation. How much security is reduced, and whether the resulting level of security remains acceptable, depend on the specific technical and operational details of the exceptional access mechanism and on the requirements and perspectives of users. Additionally, although the probability of failure associated with exceptional access may be low, the consequences can include a failure that affects many or even all users of a system or service. Quantifying the incremental risk from adding exceptional access mechanisms is made more difficult by our poor ability to characterize or measure cybersecurity risks more generally.
- *Impact on government investigations.* If exceptional access features are not provided in widely used devices and services that use encryption, law enforcement and intelligence investigations will, taken as a whole, be more difficult owing to the loss of information. Some investigations will take longer or require more resources to resolve. Other investigations will be entirely thwarted because critical evidence is unavailable. The impact on the investigation will vary depending on the particular circumstances of the case and the extent to which other investigative avenues, including the use of other sources of digital evidence, can compensate for the lost information. The impact on society when an investigation is hindered or thwarted will depend on the scope and scale of the associated crime or national security threat, which can range from undetected or unpunished commission of an individual crime to commission of a major criminal conspiracy or a terrorist plot affecting a large number of victims. Quantifying the impact of lost information on investigations or the net effect on government investigations has been complicated by a lack of systemic data and the inherent difficulty of predicting the risks of major criminal activity or national security threats.

With any proposal, one should certainly explore all the foreseeable consequences, and the framework provides a tool for doing so. Potential flaws do not, however, necessarily invalidate an option. There are unlikely to be options that satisfy everyone, and solutions will be, at best, only partially effective. Circumstances will also change over time, in ways that cannot reliably be foreseen. This is especially true for those in the United States anticipating events and trends overseas.

The framework is designed to be applicable to (1) regulatory requirements, such as a general requirement that the manufacturers of a particular device must ensure lawful access to that device; (2) policy choices, such as a decision to provide more funding to support efforts by government agencies to obtain lawful access to plaintext; and (3) particular technologies or system modifications that might be imposed by law or implemented in response to a general requirement for access. The questions that follow use the term "approach" to describe all of these.

The more specific the approach being considered, the greater the ease and precision with which the framework may be applied. This does not mean that a vague proposal is necessarily desirable or undesirable, but simply that it will be more difficult (and, in some cases, impossible) for policymakers and others to assess its desirability. This is a significant point because the stakes involve critical values to our society.

The questions that comprise the framework are as follows:

1. To what extent will the proposed approach be effective in permitting law enforcement and/or the intelligence community to access plaintext at or near the scale, timeliness, and reliability that proponents seek?

This question has four elements. The first is whether the proposed approach works to provide access to plaintext. An approach that cannot be demonstrated to work is unlikely to warrant further consideration. The second is what scale, timeliness, and reliability are needed to achieve the desired objective. For example, a lesser scale may be needed if the objective is to afford access in the more limited number of situations where critical national security interests are at stake. The third is whether the proposed approach works at the scale, timeliness, and reliability necessary to achieve its proponents' objectives. The fourth is how long the solution will be effective in the face of rapid technological change.

Some ways of obtaining access to plaintext are slow and resource intensive. These may be entirely appropriate for one-off needs. For example, the Federal Bureau of Investigation reportedly paid around $1 million in 2016 for a way to access the encrypted iPhone used by a San Bernardino terrorist. However, whether or not that was an effective approach when the government sought access to only a single encrypted device, if the goal is to provide access to a large number of encrypted communications or the content on many encrypted devices, then the proposed approach must work far more efficiently and cost effectively. An approach may not provide 100 percent of the desired access, but it needs to be worth the effort and worth the trade-offs.

Determining whether a proposed approach works at scale is often not easy because multiple components must not only be evaluated individually but also assessed for how well they integrate together. For example, a requirement that mobile phone manufacturers provide some way for law enforcement or intelligence officials to bypass encryption on devices requires not only testing the method for how well it works in real-world settings, but also assessing the tools for verifying the credentials of government officials who seek access and the tools for ensuring that access is provided only when legally authorized. In addition, evaluating effectiveness at scale also requires considering how easy it is for end-users to disable or otherwise circumvent the proposed approach, for example, by using an encrypted app or altering the device's encryption. It also involves understanding what requirements regarding robustness against skilled adversaries are practical to include, and how effective they would be. Evaluating effectiveness at scale requires not only defining what the needs are but also estimating the investment in the people, equipment, and facilities required to provide access that is sufficiently responsive to meet the needs of law enforcement and the intelligence community.

2. To what extent will the proposed approach affect the security of the type of data or device to which access would be required, as well as cybersecurity more broadly?

Given how important encryption is for the security of devices, systems, and data; the magnitude of cybersecurity threats faced in the digital environment; and how great the consequences can be of falling victim to those threats, it is critical to determine whether and to what extent a proposed approach is likely to affect cybersecurity more broadly.

This question consists of two parts. The first focuses on the specific context in which access to plaintext is sought and asks whether the proposed approach would affect the security of that particular type of communication, device, or service. This would include an assessment of what risks the proposed approach might add as well as the context of existing risks associated with the device or service. The second question asks about the broader impact of the proposed approach on security generally and is likely to be more difficult—but also more important—to answer. For example, the use of surveillance or a spear phishing attack to obtain the password to a single mobile phone poses a serious risk to the security of data on that device, but low risk to any other device. Conversely, a limit on the strength of encryption that may be provided in products and services would pose a much broader security challenge.

Answering this question also requires considering what happens in the case of failure—for example, if access credentials or known vulnerabilities are stolen from law enforcement or intelligence officials, as happened with the publication of known vulnerabilities in 2016 and 2017 that were reportedly stolen from the Central Intelligence Agency and National Security Agency. Even without a theft from a government agency, how likely is the method for gaining access to be exploited by unauthorized third parties? Is there a reliable way to cancel stolen credentials or to notify equipment and service providers of known vulnerabilities and prevent their exploitation? If the system is compromised, what is the potential scale of abuse that could occur? Is it possible to detect that a system or credentials have been compromised?

3. To what extent will the proposed approach affect the privacy, civil liberties, and human rights of targeted individuals and others?

Encryption, like all technological innovations, can be used for either legitimate or illicit purposes. Some of those legitimate uses include protecting the privacy of communications and other content. As we have seen, the law in many countries—including the Constitution in the United States—protects personal privacy. It is therefore important to consider to what extent a proposed approach could threaten legally protected privacy rights and other civil liberties.

This inquiry, too, has two elements. The first focuses on individuals who are specifically targeted by law enforcement or by the intelligence community and is concerned with how well a proposed approach ensures that government access will be permitted only with appropriate authorization and only to the content specifically authorized.

The second part of the question focuses on the privacy and civil liberties interests of people who are not targeted. How likely is it that the proposed approach could be used for unauthorized surveillance, whether accidental or deliberate, and how well does the approach guard against unauthorized surveillance? Will the proposed approach result in such greatly increased surveillance—even when authorized—that it will chill free expression or free association? Even if it is used as planned and authorized, to what extent will the proposed approach permit collection of information about people who are not targeted, including those who may be communicating with targets? Does the approach include appropriate minimization procedures or other safeguards to limit the use of communications of people who are not targets?

4. To what extent will the proposed approach affect commerce, economic competitiveness, and innovation?

Encryption has become a mainstay of commerce as a way of not only protecting the content of communications and documents, but also verifying the identity of communicating parties and of protecting the integrity of transactions, especially online. Policymakers should therefore consider to what extent a proposed approach is likely to affect commerce.

This inquiry should also consider the likely impact of any proposed approach on the economic competitiveness of U.S. providers of equipment, software, cloud-computing services, and encryption tools themselves. Will the proposed approach limit the ability of U.S. service providers and manufacturers to market their products and services as secure options or otherwise compete in other countries?

Finally, how does the proposed approach affect the ability of the scientific and technical research community to continue to advance encryption technologies or the U.S. industry to innovate in the development and deployment of new products and services?

5. To what extent will financial costs be imposed by the proposed approach, and who will bear them?

Any approach to ensuring government access to plaintext will impose costs. This inquiry focuses on the financial costs and asks, first, how great are those costs likely to be? In answering this question, it is important to consider the full range of financial costs and the full range of parties who might incur them. For example, those costs may include not only the expenses associated with engineering and design, testing, implementation, compliance, enforcement, and oversight, but also opportunity costs of customers who may go elsewhere or products and services that might not be offered.

The second part of the inquiry focuses on who bears those costs. Under some laws, such as the Communications Assistance for Law Enforcement Act, the U.S. government covered only part of the costs incurred by industry. Will that be the case with the proposed approach: Will the costs incurred by industry, individuals, and states be covered in whole or in part by the federal government?

6. To what extent is the proposed approach consistent with existing law and other government priorities?

It is obviously necessary that any approach enacted by the government comply with relevant legal requirements. Constitutional requirements cannot be changed simply by enacting a new law. More than just compliance, it is also important that policymakers consider the degree to which a proposed approach is consistent with other laws and other government objectives. For example, what would the effects of a proposal be on freedom of expression and association?

These considerations also arise in an international context. The availability of encrypted communications has been a key tool for organizing protests and resisting authoritarian governments. Support for democracy movements around the world has, at least historically, been an important objective of U.S. foreign policy. Enacting laws that would ensure government access to encrypted communications, depending on the specific mechanisms required, could conflict with that longstanding objective.

An issue related to consistency with existing law is whether unsettled questions of law may make a particular approach more challenging or otherwise less attractive. For example, policymakers may want to consider the impact of unsettled law regarding Fifth Amendment implications of requiring an individual to provide a biometric or a passcode.

7. To what extent will the international context affect the proposed approach, and what will be the impact of the proposed approach internationally?

Although laws are typically limited by state or national jurisdictional boundaries, flows of information and markets for digital products and services are increasingly global. It is therefore important for policymakers to consider both the impact of a proposed approach in the broader multinational context as well as the impact of multinational considerations on the proposed approach. For example, to what extent will a proposed approach to ensuring access to plaintext affect international trade or the quest for democracy in other countries? What would be its impact on foreign users not targeted by the U.S. government? How will it affect U.S. nationals traveling abroad? How would a proposed approach jeopardize existing international agreements around privacy and cybersecurity? For example, what are the implications for the EU-U.S. Privacy Shield Framework, which provide companies with a mechanism to comply with data protection requirements for personal data transferred to the United States?

International developments may also have an impact on the effectiveness of a proposed approach. For example, if U.S. law limits the strength of U.S. encryption products or requires that there be a guaranteed way for the U.S. government to access plaintext, will users simply switch to products and services that are not subject to such a law? Will enforcement be practical if users can download nonconforming encryption products from the Web—or implement their own solutions based on globally available knowledge? What, if any, enforcement will be necessary at border crossings to cover people who enter carrying noncompliant devices? Or will the new requirements make U.S. users communications or equipment less secure against foreign intrusion?

8. To what extent will the proposed approach be subject to effective ongoing evaluation and oversight?

Any measure for ensuring government access to plaintext is liable to be misused, whether accidentally or deliberately. The more powerful and far-reaching the approach, the greater the harm that may result from its misuse. It is therefore important that the approach be subject to effective and continuing evaluation and oversight and include a robust and assured audit mechanism that supports detection of misuse, detection of authorized use that has unintended consequences (e.g., on specific populations or international stakeholders), and degradation of the effectiveness of the approach as it is applied. This will help ensure compliance with the Constitution and other law, guard against relying on and investing scare resources in approaches that do not work, and sustain public support for any proposed approach. Policymakers are therefore advised to consider whether the evaluation and oversight mechanisms are sufficiently reliable, robust, and effective, especially in light of the breadth of their scope.

* * *

The committee anticipates that developing and debating answers to these questions will help illuminate the underlying issues and trade-offs and help inform the debate over government access to plaintext. Moreover, it is the committee's hope that the analytical framework above, together with the common vocabulary and context provided by this report, will facilitate an ongoing, frank conversation, involving all parties, about the encryption debate and proposed approaches.

Appendixes

A

Biographies of Committee Members

FRED H. CATE, *Chair*, is vice president for research, distinguished professor, and the C. Ben Dutton Professor of Law, and adjunct professor of informatics and computing at Indiana University (IU). He served as the founding director of IU's Center for Applied Cybersecurity Research from 2003 to 2014, where he is now a senior fellow. Professor Cate has testified before numerous congressional committees and speaks frequently before professional, industry, and government groups. He is a senior policy advisor to the Centre for Information Policy Leadership at Hunton & Williams LLP, and a member of the National Academies of Sciences, Engineering, and Medicine Forum on Cyber Resilience. Previously, Professor Cate served as a member of the National Academies' Committee on Technical and Privacy Dimensions of Information for Terrorism Prevention, the Department of Homeland Security's (DHS's) Cybersecurity Subcommittee, the National Security Agency's (NSA's) Privacy and Civil Liberties Panel, the Organization of Economic Cooperation and Development (OECD's) Panel of Experts on Health Information Infrastructure, Microsoft's Trustworthy Computing Academic Advisory Board, Intel's Privacy and Security External Advisory Board, the Federal Trade Commission's (FTC's) Advisory Committee on Online Access and Security, and the board of directors of The Privacy Projects. He served as counsel to the Department of Defense Technology and Privacy Advisory Committee and as chair of the International Telecommunication Union's High-Level Experts on Electronic Signatures and Certification Authorities. The author of more than 150 articles and books, he served as the privacy editor for the

Institute of Electrical and Electronic Engineers' *Security and Privacy* and is one of the founding editors of the Oxford University Press journal *International Data Privacy Law*. Professor Cate attended Oxford University and received his J.D. and his A.B. with honors and distinction from Stanford University. A former senator and president of the Phi Beta Kappa Society, he is a fellow of Phi Beta Kappa and the American Bar Foundation and an elected member of the Council on Foreign Relations and the American Law Institute.

DAN BONEH is a professor of computer science at Stanford University where he heads the applied cryptography group and co-directs the computer security laboratory. Dr. Boneh's research focuses on applications of cryptography to computer security. His work includes cryptosystems with novel properties, security for mobile devices, web security, and cryptanalysis. He is the author of more than 150 publications in the field and is a recipient of the 2014 Association for Computing Machinery (ACM) Prize in Computing, the 2013 ACM SIGACT Gödel Prize for outstanding papers in theoretical computer science, and six best paper awards. He is a member of the National Academy of Engineering (NAE), a Packard fellow, a Sloan fellow, and an ACM fellow.

FREDERICK R. CHANG is the executive director of the Darwin Deason Institute for Cyber Security, the Bobby B. Lyle Centennial Distinguished Chair in Cyber Security, and professor in the Department of Computer Science and Engineering in the Lyle School of Engineering at Southern Methodist University (SMU). He is a member of the NAE and a senior fellow in the John Goodwin Tower Center for Political Studies at SMU's Dedman College and a distinguished scholar in the Robert S. Strauss Center for International Security and Law, at the University of Texas, Austin. He is the former director of research at the National Security Agency. Dr. Chang received his B.A. from the University of California, San Diego, and his M.A. and Ph.D. degrees from the University of Oregon. He also completed the senior executive program at the Sloan School of Management at the Massachusetts Institute of Technology (MIT).

SCOTT CHARNEY is vice president for security policy at Microsoft Corporation, working with public- and private-sector organizations to develop and implement strategies to help secure the information technology ecosystem. He currently serves as vice chair of the National Security Telecommunications Advisory Committee, as a commissioner on the Dutch Commission for the Stability of Cyberspace, and as chair of the board of the Global Cyber Alliance. Prior to his current position, Mr. Charney led Microsoft's Trustworthy Computing Group, where he was responsible for enforcing Microsoft's mandatory security engineering policies and implementing Microsoft's security strategy. Before that, Mr. Charney served as chief of the Computer Crime and Intellectual Property Section (CCIPS) at the U.S. Department of Justice (DOJ) where he was responsible for implementing DOJ's computer crime and intellectual property initiatives. Under his direction, CCIPS investigated and prosecuted national and international hacker cases, economic espionage cases, and violations of the federal criminal copyright and trademark laws. He served 3 years as chair of the G8 Subgroup on High-Tech Crime, was vice chair of the OECD Group of Experts on Security and Privacy, led the U.S. Delegation to the OECD on Cryptography Policy, and was co-chair of the Center for Strategic and International Studies Commission on Cybersecurity for the 44th Presidency. Mr. Charney graduated from the Syracuse University College of Law with honors and received his undergraduate degree from the State University of New York, Binghamton.

SHAFRIRA GOLDWASSER is the RSA Professor of Electrical Engineering and Computer Science at MIT, a co-leader of the cryptography and information security group, and a member of the complexity theory group within the Theory of Computation Group and the Computer Science and Artificial Intelligence Laboratory. In 1992, she began a parallel career as a professor of computer science and applied mathematics at the Weizmann Institute of Science in Israel. Dr. Goldwasser has made fundamental contributions to cryptography, computational complexity, computational number theory, and probabilistic algorithms. She is a member of the National Academy of Sciences and the NAE and was a recipient of the first ACM SIGACT Gödel Prize for outstanding papers in theoretical computer science in 1993 and co-recipient of the Turing Award in 2012. She received a B.S. in mathematics from Carnegie Mellon University (1979) and M.S. (1981) and Ph.D. (1984) degrees in electrical engineering and computer science from the University of California, Berkeley.

DAVID A. HOFFMAN is director of security policy and global privacy officer at Intel Corporation, in which capacity he oversees Intel's privacy activities and security policy engagements. Mr. Hoffman joined Intel in 1998 as Intel's eBusiness attorney to manage the team providing legal support for Intel's chief information officer. In 1999, he founded Intel's Privacy Team, and in 2000 was appointed Group Counsel of eBusiness and Director of Privacy. In 2005, Mr. Hoffman moved to Munich, Germany, as group counsel in the Intel European Legal Department, while leading Intel's Worldwide Privacy and Security Policy Team. Mr. Hoffman served on the FTC's Online Access and Security Advisory Committee and DHS's Data Privacy and Integrity Advisory Committee. He served on the TRUSTe board of directors from 2000 to 2006, where he was chair of the Compliance Committee of the board. Mr. Hoffman has lectured on privacy and security law at schools in the United States, Europe, Japan, and China. He received a J.D. from Duke University School of Law and an A.B. from Hamilton College.

SENY KAMARA is an associate professor of computer science at Brown University. He was previously a researcher in the Cryptography Group at Microsoft Research. Dr. Kamara's interests are in security and cryptography with a focus on privacy issues in surveillance, cloud computing, and databases. His contributions include efficient algorithms to search on encrypted data, attacks on encrypted databases, and protocols for privacy-preserving contact chaining. In 2006, he was a research fellow at the University of California, Los Angeles, Institute for Pure and Applied Mathematics. In 2015, he initiated the Workshop on Surveillance and Technology. In 2016, he was named a fellow of the Boston Global Forum. He received his Ph.D. in computer science from Johns Hopkins University.

DAVID KRIS is a founder of Culper Partners, LLC, a business consulting firm specializing in national security issues. Prior to forming Culper in 2017, Mr. Kris was for 6 years the general counsel of Intellectual Ventures, a privately held invention investment company. He was also the deputy general counsel and chief compliance officer of Time Warner, Inc., the network and media company, where he worked from 2003 to 2009. In government, Mr. Kris was the presidentially appointed and Senate-confirmed head of DOJ's National Security Division (2009-2011); a senior advisor to Republican and Democratic attorneys general and deputy attorneys general (2000-2003); and a federal prosecutor (1992-2000). He currently advises two elements of the U.S. Intelligence Community and serves as an amicus curiae to the two Foreign Intelligence Surveillance Courts. Mr. Kris is co-author of the treatise *National Security Investigations and Prosecutions*, as well as the author of several other articles and blog posts. He is a director and contributing editor of the Lawfare website, adjunct professor at the University of Washington Law School, and a university affiliate at Georgetown University. He is a recipient of the National Intelligence Superior Service Medal, the Office of the Secretary of Defense Medal for Exceptional Public Service, the Central Intelligence Agency Seal Medal, the DOJ Edmund J. Randolph Award, and on two occasions the Attorney General's Award for Exceptional Service. He is a 1988 graduate of Haverford College and a 1991 graduate of Harvard Law School and a former law clerk to Judge Stephen S. Trott of the U.S. Court of Appeals for the Ninth Circuit.

APPENDIX A

SUSAN LANDAU is a Bridge Professor in the Fletcher School of Law and Policy and the School of Engineering, Department of Computer Science, Tufts University, and visiting professor of computer science at University College London. Dr. Landau works at the intersection of cybersecurity, national security, law, and policy. Her latest book, *Listening In: Cybersecurity in an Insecure Age*, was published in 2017. Dr. Landau is also the author of *Surveillance or Security? The Risks Posed by New Wiretapping Technologies* (2011) and *Privacy on the Line: The Politics of Wiretapping and Encryption*, co-authored with Whitfield Diffie (1998). She has testified to Congress and frequently briefed U.S. and European policymakers on encryption, surveillance, and cybersecurity issues. Dr. Landau has been a senior staff privacy analyst at Google, a distinguished engineer at Sun Microsystems, and a faculty member at Worcester Polytechnic Institute, the University of Massachusetts, and Wesleyan University. She has served on the National Academies' Computer Science and Telecommunications Board (2010-2016), the National Science Foundation's Computer, Information Science & Engineering Advisory Committee (2010-2013), the Information Security and Privacy Advisory Board (2002-2008), as an associate editor-in-chief on *IEEE Security and Privacy*, section board member on the *Communications of the ACM*, and associate editor at the *Notices of the American Mathematical Society*. A 2015 inductee in the Cybersecurity Hall of Fame and a 2012 Guggenheim fellow, Dr. Landau was a 2010-2011 fellow at the Radcliffe Institute for Advanced Study and the recipient of the 2008 Women of Vision Social Impact Award. She is also a fellow of the American Association for the Advancement of Science and of the ACM. She received her B.A. from Princeton University, her M.S. from Cornell University, and her Ph.D. from MIT.

STEVEN B. LIPNER is executive director of SAFECode, a nonprofit dedicated to increasing trust in information and communications technology products and services through the advancement of effective software assurance methods. He retired in 2015 as partner director of software security in Trustworthy Computing at Microsoft Corporation. His expertise is in software security, software vulnerabilities, Internet security, and organization change for security. He was the founder and long-time leader of the Security Development Lifecycle (SDL) team that delivered processes, tools, and associated guidance and oversight that significantly improved the security of Microsoft's software. Mr. Lipner has more than 40 years of experience as a researcher, development manager, and general manager in information technology security. He served as executive vice president and general manager for Network Security Products at Trusted Information Systems and has been responsible for the development of mathematical models of security and of a number of secure operating systems. Mr. Lipner was one of the initial 12 members of the U.S. Computer Systems Security and Privacy Advisory Board (now the Information Security and Privacy Advisory Board) and served two terms—a total of 10 years on the board. He is the author of numerous professional papers and has spoken on security topics at many professional conferences. He is named as inventor on 12 U.S. patents in the fields of computer and network security and has served on numerous scientific boards and advisory committees, including as a current member of the National Academies' Committee on Future Research Goals and Directions for Foundational Science in Cybersecurity. Mr. Lipner is a member of the NAE and was elected in 2015 to the National Cybersecurity Hall of Fame. He received an S.B. and S.M. in civil engineering from MIT.

RICHARD LITTLEHALE is special agent in charge of the Tennessee Bureau of Investigation's (TBI's) Technical Services Unit and supervises TBI's electronic surveillance, digital forensics, online child exploitation, and cyber investigation functions. He is an attorney and serves as one of TBI's constitutional law and criminal procedure trainers. He provides instruction to law enforcement officers in techniques for obtaining and using communications evidence in support of criminal investigations and is active in national groups of law enforcement technical and electronic surveillance specialists. He serves as a subject-matter expert on electronic surveillance for the Association of State Criminal Investigative Agencies (ASCIA) and the International Association of Chiefs of Police, and chairs ASCIA's Technology and Digital Evidence Committee. He frequently represents the law enforcement community's interest in lawful access to communications evidence at the state and national level. He attended Bowdoin College and Vanderbilt Law School.

KATE MARTIN is a senior fellow at the Center for American Progress where she works on issues at the intersection of national security, civil liberties, and human rights. The *New York Times* Taking Note blog described her as an expert on surveillance and detention, and a leading advocate for the rule of law in the so-called "war on terror." Before joining the Center for American Progress, Ms. Martin served as director of the Center for National Security Studies for more than 20 years. She frequently testifies before Congress on national security and civil liberties issues. She is also a frequent commentator in the national media and has written extensively on these issues for the past 25 years. At the Center for National Security Studies, Ms. Martin brought lawsuits that challenged government deprivations of civil liberties. She has taught national security law and served as general counsel to the National Security Archive. She is a graduate of the University of Virginia School of Law and Pomona

College. Before joining the public interest world, she served as a partner at the law firm of Nussbaum, Owen & Webster.

HARVEY RISHIKOF is co-chair of the American Bar Association's Cybersecurity Legal Task Force. He previously served as director, Office of Military Commissions/Convening Authority, U.S. Department of Defense, and as a senior counsel in Crowell & Moring's Privacy and Cybersecurity and Government Contracts groups in Washington, D.C., where his practice focused on national security, cybersecurity, government contracts, civil and military courts, terrorism, international law, civil liberties, and the U.S. Constitution. At the leading edge of many of the interactions between the legal community and the federal government and corporations, Mr. Rishikof is routinely called upon to represent the legal community at meetings and forums on national security, cybersecurity, and terrorism. Prior to joining Crowell & Moring, he was most recently the dean of faculty of the Roger Williams University School of Law and professor of national security law at the National War College at the National Defense University, Washington, D.C. Mr. Rishikof currently serves as an outside director to CBI, Baton Rouge, Louisiana, chairing the company's Government Security Committee. He is also the chair of the American Bar Association Advisory Standing Committee on Law and National Security, co-chair with Judy Miller of the ABA National Taskforce on Cyber and the Law, and a lifetime member of the American Law Institute and the Council on Foreign Relations. Over his career, Mr. Rishikof has been a member of Hale and Dorr and has held multiple positions in government focused on national and cybersecurity investigations. He most recently served as senior policy advisor to the National Counterintelligence Executive, the agency responsible for counterintelligence and insider threat management across the federal government. He has also served at the Federal Bureau of Investigation (FBI) as a legal counsel to the deputy director of the FBI focusing on national security and terrorism and served as liaison to the Office of the Attorney General at DOJ. Until recently, Mr. Rishikof also had a joint appointment as professor of law at Drexel University, teaching courses in national security and cyber law.

PETER J. WEINBERGER has been a software engineer at Google, Inc., since 2003 working on software infrastructure. After a stint at the University of Michigan, Ann Arbor, he moved to Bell Labs. At Bell Labs, he worked on Unix and did research on various topics before moving into research management, ending as Information Sciences Research vice president. After AT&T and Lucent split, Dr. Weinberger moved to Renaissance Technologies, a technical trading hedge fund, as head of technology. At the National Academies, he has been on the Computer Science and Telecommunications Board and participated in a number of studies, including one on electronic voting and one on bulk surveillance. From 2008 to 2016, he was a member of the Information Security and Privacy Advisory Board, the last 2 years as chair. He has a Ph.D. in mathematics (number theory) from the University of California, Berkeley.

B

Briefers to the Committee

NOVEMBER 11, 2016, WASHINGTON, D.C.

James A. Baker, Federal Bureau of Investigation
Matthew Blaze, University of Pennsylvania
Ernie Brickell, Intel Corporation (former)
Alan Davidson, U.S. Department of Commerce
Robert Litt, Office of the Director of National Intelligence
Paul Ohm, Georgetown University Law Center
Ronald Rivest, Massachusetts Institute of Technology
Peter Swire, Georgia Institute of Technology

JANUARY 30, 2017, PALO ALTO, CALIFORNIA

Andrew Crocker, Electronic Frontier Foundation
Jim Dempsey, University of California Berkeley School of Law
Jennifer Granick, Stanford Law School
Herb Lin, Stanford University
Bruce McConnell, EastWest Institute
Ray Ozzie, Microsoft Corporation (former)
Seth Schoen, Electronic Frontier Foundation
Alex Stamos, Facebook

MARCH 30, 2017, WASHINGTON, D.C.

Christopher Kelly, Office of the Attorney General, Commonwealth of Massachusetts
James Lewis, Center for Strategic and International Studies
Marybeth Paglino, National Domestic Communications Assistance Center

APRIL 26, 2017, WASHINGTON, D.C.

Richard Ledgett, National Security Agency
Stefan Savage, University of California, San Diego